THE

OVERLOOKED

By: Matt Thomas

Table of Contents

Foreword

This foreword is written by a guy who has never written a foreword, for a guy who has never written a book, which, I think, is a perfect example of why this is such an important book to read. Pastor Matthew follows Jesus boldly and he is always willing to take chances on people, chances that most others would not take. He is always looking for a seemingly unlikely brother to bring along on the journey of following Christ.

I met Matthew in 2012. After our initial meeting, I knew I had to get to know this brother more. I started to see his heart for the overlooked, the underdog, and the outcast, and especially for brothers in prison. I had been involved with prison ministry for several years and worked alongside many leaders in the prison system, but I will never forget the first time I attended a service in the prison with Matthew.

Matthew got up and shared his heart for Christ and for the men at the service. The entire room was listening. It was one of the few times I have seen someone speak where everyone in the room was engaged and no one was talking to their friends or getting up to do something else.

Matthew shared his story and how he was just like them. He had been locked up and he knew what it was like to go through hell and come out on the other side. He shared what God had done and was actively doing in his life and the brothers were fully engaged in what he was saying. Some were nodding in agreement, some were shocked by his transparency, and some were shedding tears because they felt like Matthew understood exactly what they were going through.

That night led to many more weekly trips to the prison. Matthew and I would drive one hour each way to be a part of two church plants he helped start on the inside through the Christ The Victor church planting movement. This is where Matthew realized his call to be a pastor and sharpen his shepherding gifts. He didn't just run the show, instead he hand picked leaders, poured into them, and then empowered them to lead different parts of the services. He took a chance on men who others might dismiss, but who he saw had a clear calling and leadership potential. As a result, each week I got to see some of the finest leaders you would ever meet lead their brothers in church. I truly hope you have the opportunity to see this at some point—it will change your life.

Matthew is dedicated and humble, and, by far, one of the greatest leaders of men in prison that I have ever witnessed. What you are going to read in the next few pages is his story and his passion. It is also full of clear help for those that are desiring to do what scripture tells us to do in Hebrews 13:3, which is to remember those who are in prison as though we are in prison with them.

I hope that your heart for brothers and sisters on the inside, which caused you to pick up this book, will be deeply stirred and increased. I pray that you find it as life-giving as I have and are excited to put into practice the practical steps he shares. Matthew is changing the way many are looking at prison ministry.

Thank you for taking a chance on Pastor Matthew and the many others that need to not be overlooked any longer.

Much Grace & Peace to each of you!

Rev. Andrew Medlen

Prologue

If you had told me, even just a year ago, that I would be sitting here writing a book, I would never have believed you! A year ago, I wouldn't even have considered making a move in that direction. But through a supernatural series of events, here we are! After hearing my story, many different people told me that I should put it down in words, and I recognized this as the gentle leading of God. Through these gentle nudges, I knew this is what I am supposed to do.

In fact, I would never have believed you if you had told me I would grow up to do any of the things that I ended up doing. And you could never have prepared me for the life that I am now privileged to live in Christ.

For most of my life, my thoughts were consumed with getting high. I was controlled by the pursuit of troubled girls, the drug lifestyle, and any way that I could break the law. There was nothing else on my mind at the time except anger, Satan, drugs and women. But God had other plans! Some of us who come from a background of alcoholism, drug addiction, poverty, and sexual and emotional abuse don't really have a plan to get from point A to point B. I had dreams and aspirations, but unfortunately now I can't even think of what any of those would have been. I do know that I was in a rehab for a short stint back when I was 14 and all I wanted to do and all I wanted to be was this crazy little gangster whose tombstone read "Crazy Suicidal." That is just where I was at. That was as high as I was taught to dream.

So, as I look back at my life I think of other people who were in my situation, or other people who are in a worse situation or even people whose situation might not even be as bad, and I see we all have one thing in common. We need Hope. There is a need for Revival, for something better. Something better than what we tell ourselves we deserve and what other people tell us we deserve.

The amazing thing about God is He shows you intentionality, and through it, He gives you purpose, and direction. He also shows you that there's something greater than yourself out there. And that He is greater than your surroundings, your situation, and your struggles. I have seen this to be true in my own life.

I again remember sitting there, having no other thought except what can I do to get more drugs? That was the scope of my whole life, and that was pretty much all I knew. I went to boarding school for a few years and managed to get my high school diploma. But had I not have gotten in trouble, and lived in that lifestyle, my mom would have never put me into a boarding school, and I never would have been introduced to Christ and had the seed planted. God was bigger than my situation.

At the boarding school I learned that I loved being able to physically work and to take my hands and do something that was positive. If there was a finished product at the end, that was even better. I did not have that dynamic growing up without a dad in the house, so this was a new and refreshing experience for me. God was bigger than my struggles.

I never understood what it was like to start something, then have a finished product at the end. This concept carried over into my life as a Christian and pushed me relentlessly to do things, and not give up until God accomplished something. Unfortunately, a lot of the time, progress was driven by my past failures, and my insecurities. Really even the birth of this book came out of a frustration for a system that I not only experienced, but a lot of my friends experienced. Now I have had the chance to experience both sides of the fence, literally, both sides in and out of prison. God was bigger than my surroundings.

I wrote this book because I have a lot of damage that I'm still working through, which means that I am probably not the only one. Like I said, the birth of this idea came from me being a convict and working with others who are convicted felons who don't understand that God has designed a great life for them still, even after incarceration. I want to sever the stigma with others in the world about prisons, and the people who are in there. This stigma is prevalent even in the church. Ministry and church planting is extremely underdeveloped in jails and prisons. If church planting was a pie, prison church planting doesn't even consist of a 5% piece.

I wrote this book to show the church both inside and outside the walls that God is bigger than our struggles, our situation and our surroundings. Ultimately, I wrote this book to remind all that Jesus spoke clearly and intentionally about prison, He sees and loves those who are incarcerated.

So, this my friends is for THE OVERLOOKED.

Part One

Chapter One: The Beginning

As I sit behind my desk in this maximum security prison where I now work, I am reminiscing upon all that's happened in my life. I think about the things that led up to this moment. I remember everything that has influenced my decision making. I think about societal structures that have invested in me whether negatively or positively. I remember mentors, and people who I have met along the way. I think about family that I have hurt, about religion and churches, about all the things that make or break a man or a woman, what propel them to become who they are. So as I sit here and think back on all these things, I want to take you back to when I was a child.

I was born to a father who had a serious drug addiction. My father was strung out on methamphetamines to the point that it ruled his life. He would not only do meth but he would also try any other substance that was available at the time. My mom on the other hand was not into drugs as much, but she was an alcoholic. So you can imagine that the two of them together were not a very good influence on their son.

I was born in Oregon in 1977. A few years later my mom moved me to Nevada. While we lived there, my dad would get so whacked out that he would lock her in the house and would do vicious, hurtful things to her. He would cheat on her, treat her like garbage and he was he was physically abusive. Eventually she had enough, and we moved to my Uncle John and Aunt Linda's house with my cousin Jay. You can imagine With all those relatives under one roof, quarters were tight, but that was where our lives could start over.

After a period of time there, we left and got an apartment in Reno, Nevada. This was in a low-income housing project area. It was the type of area where my mom would have to sit in a rocking chair at five in the morning with a loaded pistol, making sure that somebody didn't come through our door or through the window.

It was the early 80s, and the crack epidemic was extremely horrendous at the time. It's around this time that my mom's drinking increased drastically, and her behavior got increasingly worse. As her drinking increased, my respect for her decreased. I didn't listen to her, but instead I only cared about what I wanted to do. I was just angry and hurting.

About the time I was six, my mom didn't know what to do with me. She tried spanking me and disciplining me, but I still didn't listen to her. I didn't care what she had to say and I was just going to do what I wanted. She didn't know what to do with this as a single mom with barely any income working a couple jobs.

She finally got a better job and we moved out of that area into a better neighborhood. Shortly after the move, I was stealing stuff from the store they built in the field that I previously tried to burn. Needless to say, it was time to move again. This was around the time I started third grade. My mom was still active in bars and spent a lot of time out drinking and partying. Because of her partying, I would get left in a variety of places. I stayed overnight at some daycare places in the middle of the week, overnight at other people's houses, overnight at friends of hers that weren't really friends, just drinking buddies.

On several occasions, I stayed with a family who had three sons. These boys would take me into their closet and do things to me that should never be done to a young boy. I knew I wasn't allowed to say anything, and even if I could I wouldn't know what to say. So I stuffed it all inside.

This continued for a while and so it just kept eating me up inside until I was so angry all the time and felt completely alone. At the time I was diagnosed with ADD which just complicated everything even more. I didn't know how to talk. I just didn't know how to explain to anyone what was happening to me. So I just got angrier.

I didn't have a dad who was around and this just devastates a young boy. My mom had a boyfriend named Stan who was an amazing guy. However, by that point I was already acting out and didn't care. I was angry and rebellious, and just hated everything my mom and him did.

One time I ended up stealing a pair of gloves, and I came back later that day with a friend of mine to get more. He ended up stealing something else, and then I stole something else, and we got caught. It was Christmas Eve and I had to go to juvenile hall for two counts of grand larceny. My mom was at home decorating the Christmas tree, and I was getting arrested. I ended up going to court and they gave me a fine and some probation.

Another time, I was hanging around a kid who was in fifth grade and we decided to break into the school. So I wrapped my hand in a jacket like I saw on TV and put my fist through the window of the school to reach in and open up the door. We stole the money out of the library, set a fire and threw the fire extinguishers down the hall. While this was happening, the police had surrounded the school and told us to come out with our hands up. I tried to be cool and blame it on the dude who was older, but really it was my idea. They believed me and so I got out of it and ended up only doing a bunch of community service. The people in our hometown of Nevada were thoroughly displeased with me and my mom because of my actions, so we moved from Nevada to California.

When I got to California, I was a mess. I was in fifth grade, so I was still really young. However, I was warped from being abused and I didn't understand anything about sex and love at all. I had no understanding that that this type of intimate affection was supposed to be a certain way, in a loving context under God. So I fooled around with other kids when I was young, and I ended up messing around with a cousin, and we did stuff that should have never happened. My actions stemmed from hurt, but they were still wrong. I knew that there was something not right, but I was so warped, young and confused that I did not know what to do.

So later on, between fifth and sixth grade, I got caught messing around with another boy. The parents tried to press charges saying that I was to blame, but actually it was just boys doing something that they shouldn't have been doing. So when this happened my mom asked where I learned about this, and I finally told her what had happened when I was young.

She just kept saying, "Why didn't you tell me, why didn't you tell me!?" At that time, my dad was fresh out of prison and trying to be in my life. However, he was strung out and still doing multiple drugs. He actually started intravenously shooting heroin along with the methamphetamine and drinking really heavily. My dad would tell me that I was a gay weirdo, and he didn't understand how I could let this stuff go on. My own father put all the blame on me, and to this day I still deal with that pain and it tarnishes all I do. I still remember the shame he provoked in me- it is like hate and love and disgust all in one feeling.

This twisted process shaped my younger years. I wasn't even twelve and I had a heart full of sadness and brokenness. Right after I turned twelve, we moved out of the LA area, and over to West Covina. This whole time all I wanted was to be loved by my dad and to make him proud.

When I turned thirteen, my dad told me I was a man now and therefore I was going to drink with him like a man. I said, "Let's do this" and so started my journey with substances. I started drinking, partying and smoking some weed with him. We did some other drugs, and he would get me so drunk that I didn't remember much afterwards. As some more time went on we ended up moving to Fullerton in Orange County and I really started smoking marijuana and stepping into that life. It wasn't long before I tried meth for myself one night at a family friend's house.

With that first line, I finally felt normal. After all this pain, all this drama, all this everything that was going on, as the drug entered my system I finally felt okay. I knew that I had to have it, and I knew that my life would never be the same. It wasn't just euphoria, it was anger and sadness, and every other emotional memory. And then I came down for two days. You would think that coming down would make a difference but it didn't. I was already totally addicted.

I wanted to be just like my dad. I thought he was coolest thing in the world. The most awesome thing in the world to me was the biker image, drug addict, tough guy image that was my dad. So, my life became all about partying with my dad.

It got so bad that one night my mom was out of town and I had a friend come over with a case of beer to chill. For some reason, he ended up locking himself in the bathroom with his beer, so I almost shot him with my mom's gun that she had in her room. I was that desperate to get drunk.

I was hooked! I stole all my mom's stuff that was worth any value to trade for drugs. Everything worth any value, all my money, anything I could spare went to buying more and more drugs.

I was a drug addict.

Chapter Two: The Spiral

It quickly became clear how bad of a state I was in, but I really didn't care as long as I was able to get high. That's all that really mattered to me. I found myself not feeling like a whole person, just a creature. Just an outcast that no one wanted to be around or even look at. Or just something that was completely forgotten about. I only felt alive when I was high.

This carried on for a couple years. As I got a little older, there was a guy named Cracker who was in Fullerton with us. He was a dropout who had just turned 18. He had a car and he said, "Let's go do something." So we went to a town called Lynwood in California to a guy named Tavo's spot and smoked some cocaine and weed with him.

Tavo went to the store to pick some stuff up, and it turned out the car was stolen. The police came looking for us and picked us up. We ended up getting charged for Grand Theft Auto. Well, it came out later on that somebody had given Tavo the keys to the car and he hadn't actually stolen it. So we ended up not getting in trouble for it.

I met Tavo through my dad. He was my dad's friend from prison. After picking up some heroin, my dad took me down there to get me a tattoo, and to get high. That's where I got my first tattoo at only 13, and it was the first and only time that I ever tried intravenous drug use. My dad shot me up with some heroin because he wanted to make sure that I tried it at home and not somewhere on the street. Honestly, that made sense at the time, but it doesn't make much sense now. In hindsight, what happened is God had used that experience to stop me from intravenously shooting methamphetamines later on in life and really kept me away from heroin.

At around the time I turned 14, I really started messing up real bad. At this point my mom had to hide everything she owned and the gun had to be chopped up so that it I could not use it. She was living with a raging drug addict, and at the time she was a full blown alcoholic.

My mom decided it was time to get sober, so she checked herself into rehab. I remember times when I was in fifth grade when my mom came to pick me up from school, and she was staggering drunk down the hallway. This was not a good time in our lives. When she decided to get sober it was probably the best thing that could have ever happened to us. The beautiful thing about struggles and troubles, is that there's this thing called collateral beauty. However, many times you can't see the collateral beauty until you are older. But all this craziness shapes you to be who God wants you to be. It's just hard to see it when you're in the moment.

As I went through high school, I lived with a serious drug addiction. I was super skinny and was dropping acid just about every other day because it was extremely cheap. I was smoking marijuana every single day and doing meth as much as I possibly could.

In school I had no credits. I had a less than an F average so I went ahead and dropped out. The very day after I dropped out of high school, my mom decided that she is going to send me to a school for wayward boys.

It was an independent fundamental Baptist school, and they were very strict on their standards. They believed in the King James version of the Bible only, women were only allowed to wear dresses, and no other music was allowed except hymns. Talk about a culture shock. But, they showed me how to work, and I loved it. They also showed me who Jesus was, but at the time I was not ready to really understand this God thing. So all I picked up was the judgmental side or the legalistic side of what to do and what not to do. I never understood the relationship.

I ended up graduating high school through the Baptist school. I was there for around three years. I stayed a little longer to get all the credits done then I left. I tried to go to college but I did not know how to have a real life. I didn't know how to hold a job, I didn't know how to study, so I basically did not know how to be a man.

I went right back to what I knew, which was partying, getting high, and having fun. I ended up in Vegas with an aunt trying to find a job and I joined a crew that sold magazines door to door. Through this, I met a girl and started messing around with her. She ended up getting pregnant so she joined the crew to follow me, but they separated us so we left. We started living with my mom in Long Beach, and I had to find a job because I was going to have a baby. So, I joined the navy.

In the navy, I became a sonar technician on a submarine, and for the first time in my life I was doing well. However, I was not done with my drug life. I started getting high again and so did my then wife, and then I started selling drugs to all the people in my division. I could get it cheaper than they could. So, I was able to support my habit completely, and make a couple bucks on top.

Well, you can imagine, me and my wife now were full blown using, and things went downhill quick. By this time, we had two beautiful little girls, but we were living a double life. It wasn't long until we split up, and I ended up as a single dad in the navy. Praise God I eventually got an honorable discharge, which I sure did not deserve and moved to Washington. I spent nine months up in Washington just getting high. That's all I ever did was get high. I didn't do anything to take care of my kids, just got high. Out of nowhere, my ex-wife showed up in Washington, and said she wants to work it out, so we came to Arizona to unsuccessfully try to make it work.

I ended up homeless in Arizona, with no kids anymore because my wife had pulled a trick with the police to get the kids. At this time, I was staying away from all the powders and only smoking marijuana, because of course when you're in the game, you say that that's not a drug.

Then one night I did some cocaine, which meant I had to get more. I started selling cocaine, which of course turned right back into meth because that was my drug of choice.

I started working at a brake shop and made friends with my co-workers and the manager. We would work all day, and then we would run stolen cars through the shop at night. If we didn't have drugs left, the manager would say that we were robbed and then steal the deposit. Then we would go get high for the next two nights.

My life continued to spiral downhill through all of this. I got divorced and married to another woman who was also a drug addict and who would tell me, in the same breath, that I'm a horrible person and a piece of garbage, but she's tired of the kids, so I better come get them or I'm going to find them tied to the tree.

I started to get to know a friend of hers who began to show me the struggle between the spiritual world and the physical world. There were these random things that would happen in my life that were not so random. I'll give you one incident.

I was catching a bus to go to work at a temp agency, and I had to transfer from one bus to the other. I crossed the street to a bus stop, and there was a guy that looked like he had been up for a while high and tweaking for days on meth, kind of sorting through some stuff on the bench. I walked up and said, "Hey, what's up?"

He said, "Hey, how you doing?"

"I'm all right, just going to work."

I stood there for a second and then he reached in his pocket and he pulled out some meth and he looked up and he said, "Here you go Matt."

At that point, I looked in his eyes for the first time. I'll never forget his eyes. They were completely black. His pupils and everything were just black, there was no white, and there was no color.

It scared me so bad, I walked across the street and got on the bus to go back home. Of course, I took the drugs with me and did them, because even though it scared me, I was still an addict.

In 2002, I went to rehab. I went for three months, 90 days clean and sober, which is the longest I'd been clean and sober in a very long time. I was down at the Salvation Army in Tucson doing awesome. My body was solid and well-built. For the first time in a long time, I was healthy and good to go. I even got to spend some time with my children and with my mom. However, I ended up leaving and going back to Mesa, getting back together with a girl, and blowing my sobriety.

While with this woman, those random spiritual things seemed to happen more. She talked to me one time for 15 to 20 minutes and it was like there was someone else talking through her, and she never blinked. It was the weirdest thing.

There was also another incident where we broke up. I was listening to some music and fell asleep. I had this dream that I was playing with this giant dog, and I was scared but this dog just wanted to play with me. And for some reason in this dream the dog represented evil and wanted me. Well I ended up in her house later on, and she ended up telling me about my dream that I had all the way across town.

Later on in 2002, my divorce with my ex-wife was finalized, and she got custody. We had joint custody of the girls, but she took the girls and left for Kansas from Arizona and I didn't hear from her again for a long time.

That year, in November I got a phone call from my grandpa telling me to call my grandma on my dad's side of the family. So I call, and she tells me that my dad was beat into a coma, and died a week later in the hospital.

My dad got caught in the bathroom with another woman, intravenously using drugs. The woman's boyfriend woke up, grabbed a bat and beat my dad near to death, broke his neck, fractured his skull, and made my dad comatose. While this was happening, one of the girls got out of the house and called the police. The guy was calling around to have somebody come help him bury the body. My dad died a week later in the hospital.

As soon as I found that out, everything changed. I went from just using drugs and selling drugs, to robbing people, and breaking into people's houses, stealing their cars, and taking their trailers. I took everything I could, day or night to supply this habit that was ferocious and growing inside of me.

Thus, began a couple years of running around semi-homeless doing no good anywhere. I stayed with a guy for a while, then he threw all my stuff out on Christmas. We got into a fight, and I ended up cutting his cheek with a knife. Things just kept getting worse rapidly. It really wasn't long until I found myself around a group who were operating on a whole different level.

In the criminal world of Arizona, there was a just a couple of groups at the top of the food chain, and I got to kick it with them. I thought it was awesome because finally I found some identity in something.

I ended up running around with these guys for a couple of years. Come to find out, there really was no honor among thieves. At the same time I thought I was working on some kind of affiliation, they were doing all of the stuff that they kill people for. Even trying to get me set up with cartels as they robbed them in masks, while using my name so I'd get killed. You would think that would change my perspective, but it never did.

One time I stole a car, then stole a plate off of another car, and then I got caught in the stolen car with some girl in Phoenix. They arrested me, put me in jail and then they let me out a week later which was really strange. But when you're a drug addict, you don't really pay attention to what's going on around you. So, what they did was put me under investigation, so that they could build a bigger case against me, which they did.

My name was involved with theft, drug dealing, armed robbery, trafficking and a variety of other things. They kept hearing my name and kept hearing my involvement, but they could never really get something to stick that was legitimate. I went to court for a stolen car and the judge gave me six months in jail and a felony charge, but no prison time and probation. I walked out of the courthouse and immediately broke into a car at a gas station across the street from and stole all the stuff out of the car. They got me on video surveillance doing that right after I left court.

A couple of months before I went to court, I met this girl named Christina. Christina was addicted to drugs, but not a criminal. I ended up turning her from just a regular drug addict into a career criminal. We were infatuated with each other and soon we were engaged, but I was a horrible person and treated her as such. In the process of finally dealing with all of the mess I created with the court, and getting engaged, everything caught up with me and I got arrested. They got me for a generic theft charge that was not real and held me on no bond, so I could not get out. When all was said and done, they charged me for theft a means of transportation, burglary in the third degree, burglary tools, and possession of paraphernalia. Possession of marijuana came a year later. The possession of paraphernalia is funny though, because I went to jail with a baggie of marijuana and the Mesa Police Department somehow made the marijuana disappear out of the bag and they changed it to possession of paraphernalia. So think what you want, but I'm pretty sure I know what happened there.

I got three years in prison, and it was at that point that I really began to see the hand of God moving in my life.

Chapter Three: The Burden

At this point in my life, I was in Alhambra, Arizona getting ready to find out the compound that I was going to be sent to. Through this process I ran into my old dealer Steve. Steve was a solid guy. He was heavily affiliated, but had a great heart (this may sound crazy to some of you, but that is ok!).

I started talking to him in hopes of getting my ink and putting in some work on the yard. I wasn't really scared to go to prison, because I was going with all the people that I knew. Steve pulled me aside and said don't do this! He said do your prison time, get out, be a man, and raise your children. Don't waste your time with this garbage. It is not what you think. What matters is who has the drugs. It's not about your race, your skin. It's not about anything that you think it is about. It's about money and drugs. He wished me the best and from right there my life changed.

Eventually I was sent to Apache Unit, Winslow State Prison, and I was still reeling from what Steve told me. When I got there, I stuck my nose in the Bible. All I really wanted was to know God. I was so hungry for God, all I wanted was to feel and experience God, and soak up who He is. Guess what, that was not the norm for prison. The norm is extortion and pride, anger and racism, and hatred and drug abuse. All those things that got me there in the first place.

I started to work in the kitchen. Now in Arizona, it's extremely segregated – the whites with the whites, the African Americans with the African Americans, the southern Hispanics with the southern Hispanics, the northern Hispanics with the northern Hispanics, and the undocumented Hispanics with themselves, the Native Americans and Pacific Islanders are together. That's how it is divided up out there. You don't bunk with another race, you don't eat with another race, you don't mix at all with another race or you will end up in a fight.

One of the rules when I got there was whatever you do, don't get caught stealing. One time while in the kitchen, there was a Native American man who tried to get me to pass some food through the slot, and I refused. Well, he called me a punk and some other names, and he was massive, probably twice my size. I really didn't want to fight him, but I knew I had to. I didn't do anything while we were still in the kitchen, but we lived in the same housing unit, so it would happen there. I put my boots on, and I went into the closet with this dude. He looked at me and said "Man, I don't want to fight you, I apologize." And we shook hands and left it at that. I didn't see it, but God was at work changing the prison yard. He was working on taking the hopelessness of prison and doing something amazing with it.

So somehow, God blessed this yard of 440 people to where we regularly had 70 to 80 members in a church that we had planted inside of the prison on Saturday nights. Through fasting and Friday night prayer, God honored that! Soon, we were eating together with other races and having cookouts together.

We got to do these things as a church, that you'd never be able to do in the first place. We even had the heads of the yard show up to our Christmas services!

So, I did my time, and I got out of prison. I came out of prison on fire for God. God is blessing me in all things, and His love is all over me. These amazing things are happening all over the place. I got a job the second day out landing in a great spot. I was in a great situation, and I was around good people. I started working at this restaurant and then I get another job!

Then I met a girl and instead of walking with God, I walked out of church to be with this girl. She was a mess (not that I wasn't) and there was alcoholism and a lot of other problems that of course I was too prideful to see. We got together, and we started sleeping together and living in sin. And when you step out of God's will, you incur a mess of problems that He has been protecting you from, like myself and my addictions.

I blew my sobriety using some prescription drugs incorrectly. And even though I never started drinking, or got high again with the meth and the weed, I still was an addict. So, I restarted my sobriety.

I got off of parole in September of 2009. Shortly thereafter, in October on Halloween in Lyons, KS, somebody kicked the door of my ex-wife's house and stabbed her. Brutally murdering her on Halloween.

This destroyed my daughters. I had these two girls who were hurting, and I didn't know what or how to fix anything, or even help, so I drove out there. We went to the wake and the funeral. I was able to be there for them, but I was so selfish and wrapped around this girl that I was with, that I didn't move out to be the dad to my kids when I needed to be. It took me another year to do that. When I finally moved out, it was the end of 2010 and beginning of 2011.

While I had been in prison mytwo girls had been removed from their mom's custody. She was running through the house chasing my oldest daughter, threatening to kill her and to beat her up. Come to find out, there had been a whole bunch of abuse in the house continually and it had been bad for a while. So while I was in prison I had signed my rights over to my mom. The agency for that area told me that if I didn't sign my rights over I would lose any chance to know my girls anymore and that I would never see my kids again. It hurt, but I could not provide anything from prison, nor did I know how to be a dad, so I knew this was the best thing for them. I know my mom had the best interest in mind for the girls.

So, I moved to Kansas and brought the girl that I was with. I wanted to be a dad to my kids. The unfortunate fact is, this girl and I were not good together nor healthy and I hurt my daughters even more through this process. The whole situation was bad, so she went back to Arizona rather quickly.

A few months later, on a social media site, I found Christina, who was my fiancé when I went to prison. I sent her a message, and then the page blew up with her responses.

We started talking again. She said that she wanted to be with me. However, with my recent experience with the girl that just left, I was realizing that throughout my life, I was not a good person to the women that I was with. So, we agreed that it would not be a good idea for her to come out right away. She actually moved from Arizona to El Paso, just to show me that she was serious about getting together. Wow, I have never had anyone love me like that.

In my heart, I knew that I had taken her to a place that she never needed to be in the first place. I knew that I owed her everything for what I had put her through. I talked to the girls about this, since at the time I was living in my mom's basement. They thought it would be cool if she came out.

I still wasn't living right nor was I living for God. She ended up pregnant! A couple months down the road, we almost lost the baby. We went to the hospital to see what they could do at the emergency room. The nurse came in and I asked her "Will the baby make it and be ok?" She replied, "I just want to be honest with you. There's really not much that we can do. You need to ready yourself, because there's a good chance that the baby is not going to make it."

The next day I sat in a church parking lot inside of my old '76 Ford pickup and I just prayed. I said, "God, I understand I deserve this. I've spit in your face every time, and disrespected you, and treated you like garbage. I have welched on everything I've ever told you, but I ask this one time. Please don't let this baby die. I promise that we will not have sex anymore till we are married."

We didn't and we now have a beautiful boy named Hunter, who is a miraculous gift from God.

My pastor from Arizona drove out and performed the wedding ceremony in my mom's backyard in Wichita, Kansas. He drove all the way from St. John's, Arizona to make sure that we were right before God! Over the next few months, God really dug in to me, and I really sought Him like I had never before. Everything in my life changed.

I started digging into the Word deeper. I started listening to sermons whenever I could. I started downloading podcasts and sermons to a recording device while I worked at a church overnight, on third shifts doing maintenance. I submerged myself in God because I knew he had a calling on my life. I didn't quite know what that was, but I knew there was a calling.

As time went on, I felt God pulling me to work with prisoners. I didn't understand it, but I talked to Christina about it. She saw this commercial on TV about a program called *Mentoring for Success* in the Kansas state prisons. Now there's a little mystery around this commercial because they say that they never make commercials. At least that's what my trainer Sean said, but I know we saw this commercial because I was there. I believe it was God at work directing me to prison ministry. So, Christina gave me the phone number and I called this lady named Gloria, who is the amazing lady in charge of the program. I went to this training and I told the guy, "Hey I'm a five-time felon, so I'm probably not going to get approved to go in the prison." He said, "Don't worry about it, you'll be fine, I promise You'll be okay." So again, I said, "Look, I'm nervous. I'm kind of petrified, I don't know if it's going to work." They called me two weeks later and said, "Come pick up your ID. You're good to go!"

Here's where we started the walk that I'm on right now. Time kept going on, and I'm going in the prison a lot now. They kept giving me guys that were troublemakers because I had been in prison before, and it was a total blessing. It was frustrating all at the same time because I couldn't figure out why they were giving me all these knuckleheads. I just wanted a nice and easy guy that I could mentor, but what I didn't understand at the time is God was preparing me to do this very thing for Him.

I really felt God start burdening me about reentry and how these guys have nothing when they are released from prison. I decided to go to the director of missions at our church and said, "Hey, why don't we have a prison ministry? There are four thousand people here, I don't understand why we don't have a prison ministry." Martha Smallwood (one of the most amazing woman of God that I had ever met) says, "Because you haven't started it yet Matt."

God gave me a vision for what to do, mirrored after the ministry that I went into getting out of prison in Arizona. The outcome was Firm Foundation Ministries. Homes that provided men coming out of prison with a place to stay. We didn't have anything at all to start with at the time, but now there are three houses operating in Wichita, KS, one opening soon in Kansas City, KS, and one in Topeka, KS.

Well in the process of opening these reentry houses, I got to preach my first sermon in El Dorado Prison. It was five minutes, but powerful. Then I got to start speaking inside of Hutchinson Correctional Facility a lot.

We managed to plant two churches in HCF, one in the medium facility and one in the minimum facility. All the while, we were fully empowering the men who were inside. The prison church was planted and successful, only because of empowered men still in prison.

When we were about a year into it, my buddy Randy and I were talking on the phone one day when Lansing Prison came up. Lansing is the biggest prison in the state of Kansas, so naturally we thought that should be our next spot.

So, guess what ended up happening? Six months later I came up to Lansing to visit an awesome ministry named Brothers in Blue Reentry. I was there to do a couple of interviews for some guys who applied to come into Firm Foundations. While I was up there, the director resigned and some acquaintances said, "You should try for this Matt!" And I said, "Well, certain things have to happen for me to even try." Wouldn't you know it, they all happened.

I put in an application and a resume and came up talk to them. I ended up not getting the job which led down a path of uncertainty in my calling, and quazi-depression for about a month after. Of course, I began questioning myself, and asking, "What am I doing wrong? And why did God set this up just for it not to happen!"

A month of this goes by, and I get this phone call that changed my life forever.

"Hi Matt! We want you to be part of the team of Brothers in Blue Reentry. We would like you to come up and run the program portion of the ministry." And, so I did.

I really had no idea what I was doing, but I knew that that's where God had me even if I was completely unqualified. I really had no idea how to manage a giant program like that.

God had this purpose for me and my family, so I accepted it, and moved my family from Wichita, Kansas. We ended up selling the house that we owned to the neighbor across the street for a cash price. It only took two weeks! I went ahead to start working and then my family joined me shortly after. We stayed in a hotel for a while, then with a friend, then we bought a house in Kansas City.

Through this process God built into me this burden, hurt and pain for what happens in the prison system. You get a perspective or a certain view when you're in prison, and you get a different view when you visit a prison, but then you get a whole different view when you're a contract staff at a prison. Working in a prison 40-plus hours a week, watching and studying other people and other organizations, and seeing how churches interact and visit, has given me a solid understanding and a vision of how to work together and really build a model that is efficient and reproducible.

I realized that as a church we are missing a giant community of people. I realize that if you are a violent offender, or if you are a sex offender, or if you were a snitch, or if you are any of these other things that you could put a jacket on, then you've got a tough road ahead of you. Unfortunately, to the community of people on the outside of the walls, some think that all the people in prison are bad and dangerous people who will never change and need to rot in there. I have to balance this with Jesus' words when he says, "All you that are burdened and heavy laden come to me and I will give you rest" (Matt 11:28). To me that speaks to all!

I have two wonderful brothers in Christ named Troy Trussell and Troy Stallons. Neither have done any prison time, however both are pastors of churches for the Christ the Victor movement behind the walls. The beauty of this model is anyone called can do this!

These groups have successfully planted four churches inside of two penitentiaries, and one church outside of the penitentiary ran by the men who were in the penitentiary. Now we are looking at planting one outside, in downtown Kansas City, Kansas.

I used to get mad as an ex-prisoner and ex-convict. I always felt like we were left out, and that we were the last on the list for ministry. Some of you have seen this with your own eyes. Look, I understand it is not glamorous, and there is a lot of pain and broken heartedness associated with it. But I will say, Christ repeatedly speaks about those in prison. Even in Isaiah, he says He has come to set the captives free (Isa 61.1).

People planting churches for their own suburbs and not in the urban communities frustrated me. I didn't understand why they wouldn't help. They had all the resources at their fingertips and manpower to do it, but nothing would happen! Then I matured a little and had to realize, that that's not their calling. And what they are doing is fulfilling their calling where God led them.

Well my calling is to the prison. Men and women inside and out need to be empowered to live out their calling and be successful in Christ! So rather than complain about what's not happening, I need to focus on what we can do. And that is where this book comes into play.

The burden is that there are over 9 million people wrapped somewhere in some capacity in the justice system. In our pursuit to ratify crime and poverty, we have created a system of hopelessness, and a spirit of apathy about those in prison.

True change must begin with the heart. That change only comes through salvation in Christ. If we want to see revival in the world like we say we do, then we need to train the church to be prepared for such an event. Gone are the days of just giving an invitation at the end of a Bible study in the prison. This doesn't work in our home churches, so why would it work in a place where everything is pushing against any kind of right living through faith in Christ. What needs to happen is training, discipleship, and churches that prepare, and receive men and women of all walks. We say all are welcome, but then we betray that very statement with our actions.

That is why I am proposing a shift in the culture to where we are planting churches inside of the prisons all over the United States and all over the world. We need to have conferences on planting Urban Ministry churches inside of the facilities, and training on how to walk with prisoners and continue that same path on the outside.

My burden is for Revival to sweep through our prisons.

Part Two

Chapter Four: The Need

We have created an epidemic of massive proportions by packing people into prisons and warehousing them. Without Jesus, what it creates is a glass ceiling that we have already hit and shattered through. Then we reset the ceiling and break it all over again. I will never say that I didn't deserve what I got in the form of the sentence handed me for my crime. To be honest, I was not living a good life and there was a ton of stuff that I got away with. What I am saying though, is that without education, without hope, and without any knowledge of a life lived through Christ, we are doomed to keep building more and more prisons, and closing more and more schools. We will continue to let our neighborhoods and communities be filled with death and poverty, rather than abundant life.

Basically, depending on the amount of money that we have for representation, if somebody does wrong we take them out of the situation and place them somewhere to think about it for a set period of time. Please understand this book is not written with a lean to either political side. Nor is it my intent to complain about the government. This is a real problem that I personally had to face through my own incarceration and have watched in other people's.

We put them away in a fence, and don't say anything to
them. We forget them and say, "Well he or she got what
they deserved for what they did!" We don't train them,
and don't help them learn the things that might have
kept them out of prison to begin with. We don't teach
them any different behaviors, and then put them around
2,000 other people who are in there doing the same
thing. We sometimes take young children and place
them right with the 15% of the population that will
never leave, who push them to be predatory and expect
there to be change in their life. Or we give them
structures to navigate that most of the world considers
normal, yet they fail them. Since they were children, they
were told to rob, take, and never trust anyone, because
nobody really cares about them anyway.

On April 8, 1864 the 13th Amendment to the
Constitution passed. It was supposed to ban slavery and
involuntary servitude. The other outcome was an open
window for the incarcerated to perform work for
nothing, and to throw away the key after locking people
up for small offences. Unfortunately, the majority of the
people were the African Americans that had just been
"freed" from slavery. So instead of packing people on the
plantations and calling it slavery, they picked people up
on petty charges and gave them lengthy sentences and
called it prison. This cycle is perpetuated throughout the
world, but the worst of this seems to be here in America.

Now, this is not the whole prison system, nor is this the
motivation of all the government agencies and their
officials. But this is a symptom of a bigger problem. The
problem is sin. The prison system as a whole is here to
be a deterrent for us not to commit crimes. However, it

has become a badge of honor in the urban setting, which pushes kids to strive to get respect and honor through. And in the suburban setting, there are a lot of opportunities that help the kids not get into the depth of the same trouble that the kids do in the urban setting do. But guess what, THEY STILL DO!

It is a sin problem, plain and simple. The gravity of the heart will always push towards something that rests outside of the boundary that was established by God. Yes, times have gotten worse. Yes, the moral waters are far more muddied than they were 5, 10, 50, or 100 years age... Or are they?

If the Bible shows us anything, it is for certain that we as people have cyclical periods of time. That is to say that as we review history coupled with the lifestyles that we read about, I can't help but deduce that nothing really has changed, except the time that we live in and the amount of people on the earth. We scream that we are far more advanced in multitudes of areas but we still commit the same sins that were recorded in history.

With a growing population, it became necessary to separate criminals from the regular population due to the risk of letting people do what they like. and if we know anything about God we know He is loving and just at the same time. So to have a justice system that performs punishment for crimes is not a bad thing, but the fault comes in with how we run it, and what are we doing to stem the tide of the ever increasing population on a straight march to prison?

We as Christians are called to make disciples. We are also called to visit the prisoner and to set the captives free (Matt 25)! Now, there is probably not much of a chance to just proclaim "INMATE 211237 COME FORTH!" and then they get physically released. But what we can offer them is true freedom, real new life, and new hope. Real beginnings that can and will bring families back together. Real reparation to torn and broken relationships. Real sobriety and serenity. A firm foundation that you can build a life on. An actual redemption to the value that our Father believes we have, a value that we have let someone else steal from us.

I try to think about it like this. There is an epidemic break out of a worldwide terminal disease, and like any other disease, people get it whether they are "good people" or "bad people." A lot of these people though have done some really bad things that have hurt a lot of people and destroyed their lives and families, devastated neighborhoods and have disregarded their own life as trash also.

But the fact is, every one of them is dying, the good people along with the bad people. So, we quarantine all these people and pack them tightly in small groups around the world and separate them from everything and everyone they can infect. Which in reality is a safe and good practice, right?

The issue comes in the form of having the Cure, and the rehabilitation process to help them to be healthy and non-contagious and restore them to right health. Instead of looking for this cure, we don't do anything beyond quarantining the sick. We just let them die in their disease. Out of sight, out of mind. And we tell ourselves that they got what they deserve. We say, "Well, I am not a doctor... so I don't know how I can help." The result is the disease overtaking the whole world. If we would have worked together to administer the cure, it would only been as bad as the common cold. But because of our apathy, it continues to kill and destroy.

The disease is sin. The Cure is Christ, and a life lived according to His standards. These quarantine facilities are prisons filled with people dying! Physically, emotionally, but most of all spiritually. There are more than nine million people in the justice system that need a Savior and our job is to tell them about Jesus Christ.

We demand to see the crime rates drop, and the recidivism rates drop, but the only way this happens is through a heart won to Christ, and a retraining of how to live a life that is well pleasing to God. The only way this happens is by us Christian men and woman doing what Christ told us to do. We must actively pursue these people in the justice system, just like we do on the outside, when we pursue ministry.

My heart breaks watching men and women continue to go back to their old ways because there are so few laborers. We hold revivals and shows in prison that walk men and women into the presence of God, but then we do nothing else except plan for the same event the next year and the next year also. We see 500+ salvations a year WHICH IS AWESOME!!!!! But the sadness comes when we as Christians don't take the time to walk with them through the drugs, through the sexual deviance, through the hate, through the orphan spirit that rests on them, through the pain of years of family dysfunction that has worn them down to where they believe that they are not any better than the trash that they let consume them. Friends, these are souls that need Christ. These are children that are running around homeless and parentless.

God's work is the salvation of souls, our job is the guidance of souls to Christ. This involves bringing them into a relationship with Christ, but also helping them learn to navigate life and become closer to Christ through it all.

I have five children. Three daughters, and two sons. My two oldest girls are grown up, and out on their own. The third daughter I have never met, and she probably has no idea who I am. The oldest have witnessed seen their father strung out on drugs, committing crimes and then going to prison for those crimes. They watched me get out of prison and still be racist, mean to others and generally treating people like garbage. They have seen all this and this has shaped them. Then Christ came into my life. They watched their dad quit the attitude. They watched that ignorance and hatred leave. They saw how Christ placed a compassion in my heart to people and for people that was never there before. They saw me submerge myself in the work of God and in the redemptive gift that God gave me. But it wasn't until after I had caused a lot of damage emotionally and spiritually.

I also have two little boys who have never seen dad do any of those things. They have seen me grouchy and possibly a little mean every now and again, but the racism is gone. The drugs are gone. The crime is gone. The devastating overarching problems are gone, because Christ found dad.

Now imagine where my children would be without Christ in my life. The girls had a really rough patch in high school. The one tried to kill herself and the other one overdosed in the bathroom on some opiate pills, but they managed to pull through and I can't account that to anything else but Jesus Christ.

To understand the depth of the healing power that can come from Jesus Christ in a prison setting, you really have to think about the lie that has been playing and replaying in the heads and hearts of the incarcerated. The feeling of hopelessness is deep and ingrained in the lie told by the devil. When freedom comes, it is like an ocean quenching the fires of hell.

One of the major problems is that prison ministry is messy. From a first world perspective, it is definitely not glamorous. You will have people who go back to committing crimes. You will have people that will go back to drugs and drinking. Unfortunately, you will even have people that will kill themselves or kill other people.

But.

You will also see men and women have a drastic, life-changing situation when they come into contact with the Sovereign God, Creator of everything. The United States has many prison filled with men and women who have never been told that they can be successful. We have done a bad job as the body of Christ showing them a wholesome life that doesn't include crime and despair, and then walking with them through that new life. Maybe they have been told once or twice but there's no depth of understanding because if your whole paradigm is poverty and drugs and abuse, that becomes all you know, and that is all you understand. Until you come into contact with the power of Christ.

The bigger question is, how will they see that power, and how will they know that power, unless you present it and share it with them? Unless you share what has happened in your life, these men and women will remain in a place that is hopeless. Prison is a hopeless and predatory environment. It is a "what can I take from you, to make my day better" environment. But in this ugliness of concrete and barbed wire and stabbings and all this other stuff that is just plain scary, are men and women who are people who deserve to know who Jesus is. They are people who deserve a chance to receive a Savior.

We as Christians have an obligation to spread that gospel around the world. We spend thousands and thousands of dollars to go to other poverty-stricken, dangerous and corrupt places for a week across the world. We have secret churches that spread the gospel to countries that hate Christians, where death is an ever-present danger.

But we have prisons in our backyards that we neglect. We have men and women who are incarcerated right now down the street. Men and women in and out of jail who we don't spend any time with. We have kids growing up in drug-infested houses, and gang-infested houses, in the inner city and even in the suburbs. We have parents who just don't care about anything who need to know who Jesus is. Both parents and kids are on their way to prison, and we seem to neglect this whole piece of the pie.

From experiences of being involved in two different prison systems, going to prison in Arizona, then working in Kansas. I have seen a lot of hope, and many lives changed. I've seen convicted murderers give their life to Christ, get a degree, and become famous photographers. I watched other ones come out of prison and become vice presidents of companies. I watched other ones start their own companies. I've watched all these things happen, but it all started at the point of meeting Jesus Christ. And so how can we show them Jesus Christ if we're not willing to step foot inside of these facilities?

What never ceases to amaze me is that almost everyone who I run into is somehow related to a man or a woman that is currently incarcerated or has been incarcerated.

Every day, we have an interaction with someone who has been involved with corrections in one form or another. This is obviously a major problem. This is also not changing or getting better. If we don't step in as Christians to do something who else is going to do it?

We have to suit up, lace up our boots, and get ready to step on the mission field. God has called us to be a people who are holy and righteous and who take back ground that the devil has stolen, the very playground that he operates in.

It is a concentration of evil sometimes inside of prison, but that is no match for the power of Christ. We have to put on the armor of God, and step onto that battlefield knowing the victory is already ours in Christ.

Chapter Five: The Misunderstanding

There are many misunderstandings surrounding prison ministry and prison in general. It would appear that the majority of people believe that prison is a place for the worst of the worst. That it is the place where all the bad people go. At least, that's what we tell our children in hopes of them not going down that road. And overarchingly, this is how society presents corrections to the population. It is a weird thing if you think about it. A person commits a crime, even if it is committed out of addiction, or fear, or even if it is petty theft. The population as a whole, rallies around the injustice of somebody breaking a law, and screams punishment and justice!! But we are the same people that speed down the street, and cheat on our taxes. We run red lights, and some of us look at inappropriate stuff that enslaves young girls and boys.

Prison, if I am not mistaken, is a place for correction, and a time away from the public due to a crime that you have committed. It is unfortunate that in the same concept, we have built this stigma around prisons that makes it almost impossible to do anything positive and life changing for the inmates while they are in there. This makes it near impossible for any of them to be successful upon release.

We have to completely shift our perspective to understand that the punishment is the length of time in the prison, not the treatment inside of the prison. In prison, you're away from family, from friends, and everything that you know. You do the same thing every single day and it's not much.

We have warehoused people for years now. They say that in the last four decades, our need for capacity in prisons has quadrupled. The majority of the population inside prison are there on minor drug charges, or theft, DUI's and other non-aggressive, non-person charges (see appendix one for statistics). I'm not minimizing any of this, but I want you to understand all of us are capable of making these same decisions. Especially if we grew up in homes where this behavior is encouraged. I would venture also to say, some of us have done a lot of these things ourselves that put people in prison, and we just happen to not get caught doing those things.

There's a stigma attached to somebody who is a convict. This stigma follows them around for the rest of their lives. It is a giant billboard that says, "I am a bad guy, and I need to make you all aware of my wrongdoings." More times than not, this stops them from having chances in society to be successful. Now, there are a couple exceptions to this, if someone has some sexual deviance that is a repeated behavior, it is good to know where they stand, and how to avoid putting anyone in situations, including them, that would cause harm. But that still doesn't mean that they shouldn't be able to start a new life in Christ.

However, the opposite usually happens. They come out of prison with no money, no skills, no anything, and very few want to give them a place to live or a job. Or if they can get a place to live, it ends up being in neighborhoods that are not conducive to successful living. It is sad that the majority of people don't want to give them a chance at a career, or really believe that they have paid their debt.

Working as a contractor in the prison, I see a lot of guys who aren't bad guys. I see a lot of guys who don't fit the mold of predator or heinous super criminal, that will have a jacket for the rest of their life.

I am going to talk a little bit about a topic that makes a lot of people uncomfortable - sexual offenses. Not all offenses are a crazy predatory situation that involves kidnapping, murder or rape. And not every offence is a molestation case like on TV that pushes people to generalize and put every type of those offenses into one bucket.

I have seen an 18-year old kid with a 15 year old girl who have grown up together, and it just so happens that he makes the parents mad, and even though they have been together for a long time, the parents report it now, and the boy goes to prison. He comes to prison and they pick on him, they beat on him. They treat him like he's worthless. They treat him like he is the scum of the earth. They take his food and abuse him because he is a "sex offender." The sad thing is, he is just a kid that made a bad decision.

Now there are worse cases, I'm going to share one with you. There is a guy I'm going to call Joe. Joe had a brother who was a little older than him and a mom and a dad. When he was young, his dad left his mom stranded and struggling with her with two boys. The mom ended up becoming heavily addicted to a variety of drugs and drinking all through the day. The loneliness led to having a steady stream of guys and women running in and out of the house doing drugs, partying, and doing a variety of different sexual stuff. This wrecked these two boys' childhood, because the mom blamed dad leaving on the boys. Men and woman would come in and out and use the mom like she was a rag to use up and throw away.

Soon a different set of people started coming in, and the men would come into the house to sleep with their mom, but then they would stop off at these two boys' room and take advantage of them also. This kept happening over and over again. Joe's older brother would try to keep the guys from getting to his little brother by doing things with them, and eventually ended up contracting AIDS and died trying to protect his little brother.

Now when Joe got older, Joe did something really bad that he shouldn't have done. He is now a sex offender and is sitting in prison right now. I'm not saying that Joe is innocent by any means. What I am saying is there is a bigger story to Joe than his prison number.

When I heard him tell his story, it wrecked me. Even writing it down and recollecting it wrecks me. But it helped me to understand more about people in prisons who have done some pretty heinous things. What we do is throw them away, then throw the book at them and act like they are nothing because of their offense. When in actuality, they are as much a child of God as we are. They deserve to be loved and shown the grace of God and have a chance after prison. They deserve to have a life again and have the rights that any of the rest of us would have when it comes to needing counseling and growing from the situation they were in.

I've seen people come from completely different backgrounds from both sides of the tracks, wealthy and poverty stricken. It is no respecter of persons at all. I've seen kids that grow up in what most would consider an almost socially perfect environment, and still end up in prison.

I've seen them start using drugs at an early age and start stealing from the parents. To say that only a certain class of people are affected by this would be a lie! Sin is sin, and like I said it is no respecter of persons. We will find sin and brokenness in any household. All the way from the worst household anybody could grow up in, to the most extravagant and best resourced.

Even the best parenting and nurturing will still not compare to the nature of sin. I have worked with young men who come from a phenomenal family, where their parents loved them, and cared for them and still one of the kids ended up in prison, while his sister ended up with scholarships all the way through school.

We have to understand that when you strip everything else away, we are dealing with the same issue. We are dealing with a broken heart. We are dealing with a problem that is the biggest epidemic in the world. And that is Satan, and the sin nature and the brokenness inside of us.

If you set up the right situation, and the right kind of symptoms for sin to occur, you would be surprised what could happen. And it is startling what we as people are capable of. I've heard it told, "I would never do that!" Or, "I would never go that far!" I've heard that for a variety of things - I would never steal, I would never look at that stuff, I would never lie to my wife or cheat on my spouse. All these I would nevers. And sadly, I've seen them happen in just about every situation. If you're doing drugs, if you're tired and stressed, if your family is this way or that, if you are an alcoholic, if you are drunk, if you are in a state or condition to make poor decisions, you'd be surprised how easy it is to do something that could get you thrown in prison.

In closing this chapter, I understand that sometimes we don't like to acknowledge these truths, and I know I get passionate when I explain the plight of the hurting. But it is important for us to see that prison affects everybody. It affects our communities and neighborhoods.

The outside of prison feeds the people into the prison. It also feeds the drugs, and all the contraband that ends up inside. It also feeds the prison young men and women trying to make a name for themselves, who will do just about whatever it takes to be accepted. What leaves the prison is decisions for gangs, kids that become dangerous kids and come out with marching orders into communities to do no good. What else leaves is a mass of traumatized people who have never been loved and educated on how to really live a life close to Christ that is successful and redemptive.

There is more to these men and women than meet the eye, and if you change the prison yard, you change the family, and then the neighborhood. Then you have a community that will see revival because the clout of the men and women that run them have come to Christ.

So, please understand that not everybody who goes to prison is a bad person and not everybody coming out of prison is looking to recommit crimes.

Chapter Six: The Hope

I have the pleasure of working for an organization by the name of Brothers in Blue Reentry. We are a non-profit Christ-based ministry that operates inside of a prison facility. We get our origins from a larger ministry that created a program which offered 18 months of programming while incarcerated to help educate and deal with life-controlling issues that plague men and women in the correctional system. Inmates learn leadership skills, and how to be parents. They also learn how to live a life that thrives in Jesus Christ, not only when they are released into society, but right where they're at in prison. The outcome of this change is a paradigm shift in the population from hopelessness to hope and from strife to peace.

Well, tough times came to this organization in 2011, and they had to close a majority of the programs that were operating in different states, one of these states being Kansas. So, Brothers in Blue Reentry was birthed out of that change.

I get the pleasure of being the program manager of this ministry. What this entails is making sure that the teachers have the books they need to teach the classes, and that there are teachers in all the slots. Also, to make sure that the departments are following protocol. I also help handle the disciplinary procedures with staff and inmates. But my favorite part is, I get to disciple the men through hard times, and really walk through the fire of living in prison with them. I also get to help raise up leaders in Christ who will raise up other leaders!

One thing I will say to you who are looking to do ministry in a prison facility, do not underestimate the potential for an attack of spiritual warfare when you step into the prison system. In an earlier chapter I spoke of prison as the enemy's playground. It is a kind of a nexus, a concentration of hopelessness. So, through this, prisons will only get darker and more hopeless if we don't step into that darkness, with the only light that will illuminate and overpower this darkness. That light is Jesus Christ.

In Bothers in Blue, we take these men from all over the state from different prisons and bring them to our facility. We also take quite a few that are already there, and place them together into a cellhouse, to help with the growing of the "community mindset." Then we hand them a Member's Handbook to read through and study before they make a commitment, so that they understand what is required of them to be in the program, and what benefits they receive while inside of the program.

After they have gone through orientation, signed the Handbook and committed, they begin the 12-month general study curriculum. We cover our curriculum in a variety of series - the Leadership Series, the Spiritual Series, The Substance Abuse Series, the Manhood Series, the Character Series, and the Reentry Series.

It is through these 12 months that we really get to know these men, their stories, where they came from, and what they want to do in life. Not everyone will make it.

Not everyone wants to be a pastor or run some type of ministry. But... BUT, if you can pull one soul from falling in the pit of Hell, and that one person accepts Christ, there is no telling of the amazing things that can happen from that one testimony.

There are a lot of people that step up to the plate who want to do something different with their life. They are sick and tired of the way they are living, and have spent so long living the other way, losing family, losing kids, losing freedom, and they're just absolutely tired of it, ready to move forward without ever looking back!

Now, this is not the majority, and this doesn't happen in every case. There are a lot of people who still want to hang on to their sin. But the beauty is the hope.

The hope is that a seed will get planted, and that one man will see Christ, and come to know Him. The Hope is also that we can change the outcomes of the men and women returning to society, which will also affect the multitudes pouring in.

So, let's say you go on a missions trip overseas, and you get that one convert who accepts Christ and gets so excited that he tells everybody else around him. That one person is an indigenous leader who will change the people around him. He may become a pastor or a co-laborer for the coming Kingdom of God. Guess what? It is the same in prison.

Working in the prison, I have a unique perspective to see a lot of things that most people don't see. I also have a deeper understanding from my time in prison, that shapes a clearer more 360-degree view. There's a shrewder way to handle things inside than we have been doing, and there is a more efficient process, that can get a lot accomplished on the yard level.

What I mean by yard level is, you have three cultures operating together at the same time that overlap in many ways.

One culture is the society that we live in which governs who goes to prison, and for what. It may seem like it is over once they are in, but it is not. There are appeals, false imprisonments, extra charges, and then probation and parole upon release. There are also volunteers and mentors who come in to spend time with the incarcerated. And let's not forget, family and friends who come to visit, and put money in their accounts for the inmates.

The second culture is The Department of Corrections, or the Bureau of Prisons. These are the governing agencies that control the facilities and are the ruling factors for how the day to day operations run while inside prison. The Corrections Officers are part of these structures. They are responsible for the security inside of the facilities and the transport also.

The third culture is the inmate population. Even though Corrections is ultimately responsible for the rules, the only way that all this works on the day to day level is through the men who run their own mini-populations amongst themselves. It is truly like little villages that live close to each other, even using the same area for hunting and gathering, but do not cross very much because of tradition and harsh punishments.

The three coexist and co-mingle in a tight-knit, super small area that is overcrowded and under resourced.

The reason that I am writing this book is in hope of Revival in the prison system. If you have Revival on the prison yard, you will change the multitude of cultures that reside there. When these cultures change, the dynamics change. Such as, the violence will de-escalate, the extortion and predatory behavior will almost disappear. Most importantly, the inmates will have the freedom to pursue Christ without retribution from the ones in charge of their people groups.

When the culture changes, the rules that the inmates use to govern each other will be less punitive, and more geared around growth and understanding. What I mean by this is, instead of everyone getting beat up or stabbed, or being removed from the yard in an ambulance, the population will attempt to talk and negotiate things rather than go straight to the worst. I am not saying this still won't happen, because it will. It will just be way less frequent.

There will also be less of a likelihood of men getting hooked on drugs, because there will be less interest. You will see a complete shift in the attitude towards the officers. The most beautiful thing to me is when someone who has a reputation and power of their people surrenders their life. Then they start bringing almost all their people to Christ, and start promoting educational growth.

Like I said, I'm not saying that all the bad is going to stop all the way. It is still prison. But you could drastically change how things happen at that prison. The other side of the hope coin is, 80 to 90 percent of the people in prison are getting out one day. We want to see these men and women return to a community as givers, and not only show they're different, but help others not venture down that road.

We want them to raise kids in the right direction. And to teach people the dangers of drugs, and the dangers of gangs, and the things that impacted their life, to put them in the place where they went to prison. This is the Hope.

We have shut our eyes and our ears to ideas that promote growth opportunities in facilities. It is an out of sight, out of mind type of situation. What actually happens when somebody goes to prison, and Christ doesn't get ahold of him, somebody else will. And believe me, the enemy is here to steal, kill, and destroy.

So, when these kids go into prison and they're young and impressionable, they sign up with gangs and with people who use them. And instead of just doing some petty crimes they find themselves getting into extortion, attempted murder, and possibly even murder. All because they are seeking acceptance and status. The other part of the driving force is they don't want to get stabbed or get beat up themselves! So, they end up doing these things that sometimes gets them life in prison, a new felony charge, and extra time. Not to mention the PTSD in their life caused by the trauma of that lifestyle.

This is not the case in every place or prison, but this is the reality of the current culture. Without Christ, this will only get worse.

That's how important this Hope is. I am not just talking about changing them when they come out, I am talking about changing men and women on the inside while they're still in prison. This will have a major effect on the people who are still in prison with them, and they will disciple each other into the Kingdom and throughout life! I've seen it happen firsthand.

There are guys in the Brothers in Blue Reentry Program who are doing life sentences in prison. They have been passed over and over again for parole. Some have already served 35 to 40 years in. And instead of moping and sitting around, or doing drugs and hurting others, they are praising Jesus, raising up the younger generation in the faith, making sure that that they don't venture off into substance abuse and making sure that they don't return after they release.

We have men in prison, holding other men accountable to live according to Christ. I can't think of a better hope than that. These will be the same men who will come out and change the whole paradigm of what it is to be an ex-convict.

Once again, my point to all this is, if you want to see real change in communities and neighborhoods and areas that you deem bad neighborhoods, this is the sure way to do it.

In the United States we have taken prisons and made them work camps. We take these guys and work them for next to nothing. I remember being in Arizona and working on a firefighting crew doing wildland firefighting. I was making a dollar an hour! I believe the state made $14 an hour. But when you're in prison, it is the greatest thing in the world! And when you're in prison you're conditioned to be excited about a dollar an hour and leaving the prison compound to go work. I did the crime and rightly so, I should have done a ton more time. But imagine what we could do if we use these camps to train men and woman to be leaders, teach and educate them for success, in and out of school. What if we introduced them to Christ and His path and helped them save and plot a course for their lives from incarceration to incredibility. There is a massive group of men and women who are simply thankful that somebody appreciates them.

We have built a system that takes advantage of people and their situation, but it's not just the prison system, it happens on a regular basis in the daily life of returning offenders. Whether it is a company, a landlord, or the judicial system, you have an extremely rough time ahead of you as a felon. Could you imagine how the workforce would be changed by hiring these men and women and giving them chances to succeed in feeding their families to be part of society? What if above all we loved and appreciated them, welcoming them home knowing they have already paid the punishment for their crime.

There's a gentleman by the name of Randy Reinhardt who runs a company named Zephyr. I have seen him walk with guys who are in prison and treat them like family. He hires them in prison, and trains them in a trade that they can use for the rest of their life. He treats all of them with dignity and respect. He is understanding and patient as a company owner with guys who have done a lot of time in prison and have become institutionalized.

He's also taking guys when they are released and have kept them employed at his company and put them in positions of authority. Most people wouldn't do this for somebody coming out of prison.

I tell you all this to say that there is a giant group of people who have no idea how wonderful they really are. We talk about unemployment, and we talk about the war on drugs, we talk about the war on poverty, and crime. We talk about breaking systemic issues that plague us as a people, but what do we do besides complain and debate about them? We have the power of God inside of us, are we really doing the best we can?

You can do a lot in the prison as a person who has never gone to prison. And we can accomplish a lot as a people who visit and mentor. But the most empowering thing you can do for those inside of those walls is to train them in Christ and accept them fully as they get released. This is the key to successful lives who lead the community and change.

In the next chapter I will share with you some stories of changed lives. Please pray as you read this and share in the Hope.

Chapter Seven: The Stories

I would like to take a moment and share a few stories of some of the greatest people I've ever met. I'm going to start with my wife.

Christina

Christina was born in South Carolina and grew up in Tempe, Arizona. It wasn't in a best neighborhood, but a good one nonetheless. She had a young mom who was not addicted to drugs, and wasn't physically, sexually, or verbally abusive.

However, Christina started rebelling and started drinking. It didn't take too long to realize she was an alcoholic.

The alcoholism led to smoking marijuana which led to other things. As she got older, she got hooked up with an older guy who treated her like garbage. He abused her, talked down to her, told her she was stupid, pushed her around and beat her up.

She got in contact with her father who lived in Texas and wanted to go and meet him. She ended going to Galveston to meet and talk with her dad. She stayed there a while, met a guy, got pregnant, and her dad kicked her out.

She called her mom to tell her she was pregnant, and her mom came and brought her back to Arizona. She had a beautiful baby girl and named her Glenna after her uncle Glenn who had passed previously.

After Glenna was born and still little, Christina got back with another guy and tried meth. She got hooked. Due to a bad relationship and bad choices, her mom adopted Glenna, and Christina was again homeless. She ended up going back to Texas and met a guy named Jeff. He was a hard-working guy who didn't do drugs, but drank a lot. But he was a good man to her, and a good man in general.

One night they were on his motorcycle in the dark, and they slid off the gravel and hit a culvert and flipped the bike. She was thrown off, and he hung on. He died that night, and she lived. This destroyed her.

She moved back to Arizona and started spiraling out of control. She got back with the guy she did meth with, and really just gave up on life. A year later by chance she met a guy who was also strung out on meth. Except this guy was not a good guy. He was a thief, and a small time dealer. He was abusive and narcissistic. Instead of just doing drugs, he was also committing major felonies. There were stand- offs with weapons, meth labs and a variety of other crimes happening.

It wasn't too long after this that he got arrested. He went to prison for three years, and left her in the middle of a pile of thefts, stolen goods, and people who wanted to get back at him.

She ended up meeting a lady who she stole a car from and went from Mesa, AZ to Kingman, AZ. She got caught in the car and went to jail. After she got out she ran around from place to place. She ended up pregnant again, and the guy was in no place to help and neither was she. She gave the baby up for adoption to an amazing couple. His name is JT, and he is wonderful and loved.

During this time though, there was a guy that wanted to hook up with her, and she kept telling him no. One day he snuck up on her and kidnapped her. He held her hostage for a week brutalizing her while she was tied up and keeping her high and out of her mind. Nobody knew where she was, but by chance a friend thought he should check this guy's place. He found her and saw what was happening. He saved her and took her to the hospital. She spent a couple of months there getting checked out and resting.

As time went on, Christina was now tattered and torn emotionally and physically. So she moves back to Tempe where it all started.

Meanwhile, since she did a lot of jail time, she doesn't have to go to prison. They issue her a DOC number in AZ, and put her on probation and parole with a presumptive sentence. She eventually ended up in prison for a couple months, then was released and lived in Phoenix.

After she got clean, she found an old boyfriend/fiancé (me) on a social media site and got together with him. As time went on she got pregnant, we got married, and we have dedicated our lives to serving Christ, and His Kingdom.

Together we have had the privilege of seeing many come to Christ, and over five churches planted inside and outside of the prison, and have gotten to serve in a multitude of ministry opportunities!

Jack

I want to tell you a story about a guy we will call Jack. Jack was adopted when he was young and was raised in the high desert of Arizona. He was an extreme child and very athletic. He was a very hard worker, and very popular.

Jack did well throughout school, played football and had no problem being able to do the work. His character on the other hand was lacking. What looked like an amazing young man who had everything together, was just a broken little kid. Jack was raised by an old Baptist preacher who had adopted kids before and loved them no differently than his biological ones. His wife was an amazing teacher who has the patience and love of a saint.

As Jack got older, the cracks started to show with the half-truths that he told. One night he met a girl outside of a party and they got together and had sex. It turned out that she was under age, and the parents were influential people in the community, so they pressed charges.

Jack was now a sex offender, and was now on intensive probation in a small community where there is no economy. He was unable to find a good job or do anything to pay his bills. What ensued after this is a young man feeling stuck who had to make money in order to pay probation fees. He turned to scrapping metal and started running around with somebody that he shouldn't have been running around with. With this bad influence, he ended up stealing stuff from someone's yard. I'm not saying he is innocent in this, but I'm also certain that if he would have had other avenues to take he would have taken them. So they end up getting charged with burglary and Jack served prison time, getting three years for the burglary charge.

After Jack got out of prison, he returned to the small community with even less of an economy, but this time he is on probation and now parole. Because of these issues, he started to do drugs.

What we see is the revolving ball of problems that occur in people's lives inside of a system that is not conducive to learning, or growing, or seeing new things. He spent three years in prison and didn't get to do anything that would change his life for the better.

Now he has gone through rehab and is living in a sober living environment. He's working a job where he has to travel around the state, but eventually the addiction kicks back up, and he is incarcerated again for two pills that he was not prescribed, and is looking at more prison time.

Joe

I want to tell you about my friend Joe.

When Joe was 16, he moved to a different state from Los Angeles, where he grew up in the gang culture. As he was raised he was told that the police were horrible, and they're just out to kill you, abuse you, and throw you in prison. Joe was told that if you talk to the police, you deserve to die. This is what he was raised in, he was taught from a very young age to live by this culture and creed.

He was taught that if you are part of his gang it is all good, but if not, and you're in another gang, you deserve death. That your enemy is your enemy, and there is no other way.

Joe moved to a different state with different people, and the gang he was involved in grew like wildfire. As he grew up, he ended up stealing a car and getting in trouble because he had some marijuana. He told the police that he was selling it because he didn't want his mom to think he was smoking it.

The police ended up taking him for selling drugs and stealing the car, and Joe went to prison. Of course, part of his same crew from the street, and all the guys that he looked up to growing up were all sitting in prison. So he did what he knew and he got involved in the gang on the inside. He spent the majority of his sentence in solitary confinement.

After his sentence, they released an angry young man back into society, and they don't teach him anything that has to do with reentry. They just expected him to get out and be successful, or they expected him to fail. They released him out of segregation with all this pent-up anger and rage, and he ended up taking somebody's life and now has a life sentence.

He went right back to prison and did what he's always done. He put in work for the gang. This means he was running drugs and beating people up, even to the point of killing people. It also means riots and extortion. He put in this work for a long time and ended up getting to a point to where he's running the show.

One day Joe came into contact with Christ, and it changed his life drastically. Joe is still in prison and he still struggles with all of this that has been all he ever knew. He also still makes a lot of mistakes.

However, God is slowly pulling back Joe's layers and Joe is slowly changing. His people aren't just beating and killing anymore, nor are they extorting other people. Almost all the youngsters that are running around through the prison have been encouraged by him to seek Christ and education so they can be successful. He's using his power, and his influence to help them to learn about God and to learn other ways to cope besides drugs.

He is using what he has to benefit the Kingdom of God and to teach men inside that there's a better way.

Jared

I want to tell you a story about Jared.

Jared didn't grow up in the best part of town with the best family, but he had a great father who taught him a lot.

He grew up to be a phenomenal worker, who was making great money. But there was a lot of dysfunction under the surface that found its way to the top through addiction.

One night at a girl's house, who was a dear friend to him who he grew up with, a guy comes over trying to rob the house. Jared with a few other people come over and confront the guy and beat him up really bad. One of his hits ends up killing the guy, so Jared gets 16 years in prison for second-degree murder.

Around six or seven years into the sentence, Jared has an experience with Christ. This changes the trajectory of his life forever.

Jared starts reading everything he can possibly read about God and theology. He enrolls in The Urban Ministry Institute for his degree. He also starts working together with a couple other brothers in a maximum security prison to build up the church.

These men take a church that was only having around 15 people show up and through their leadership attendance grew to over 100. They start prayer outreaches, church history lessons, and build a fellowship.

Jared and another brother who is in for murder get a lower custody, and transfer to a different compound in the same facility.

They start a Bible study on the yard, and welcome all who want to come. This Bible study group also grows and they feel led to plant a church. So they reach out through Jared's wife on the outside, to my wife and to me, and ask if I want to be the pastor of this church they are planning. Through prayer and guidance, and the calling, I say yes.

What ended up happening was nothing short of a miracle. Jared got his minimum custody and got transferred. We ended up with two church plants started at the same time. Right now in the Hutchison Prison, there are two full-fledged churches blossoming inside the prisons. These are all ran and handled primarily by the men inside, and one volunteer that oversees the call out.

This is how you have prison yards getting shaken up in Christ! You have the men that call the shots occasionally checking out church, because of a little bit of obedience, and a lot of Christ.

We've seen lives and prison compounds changed forever.

Luke

Last but definitely not least, I'll tell you about Luke.

Luke grew up in a small town in a rural part of Kansas. He was the son of a farmer/rancher. From the time he was young he understood what a work ethic was, and how to accomplish and achieve a good day of work taking care of the animals on the farm. He was also very intelligent and did fairly well in school.

Luke did a little bit of partying, but nothing too crazy. He had a wonderful family that wrapped around him and supported him with a ton of love and care.

As he got older, people dear to him were getting their land and their whole livelihood stolen by a corrupt banker. This banker would take advantage of the people and their land and leave them no other option but to sell it.

So, one day he and some friends take a gun that wasn't loaded, and go to this guy's house. They basically say, "You are not going to take advantage of us anymore!" Of course, the guy calls the police, and Luke not only gets hit with state felonies, but federal offenses also. The guy owned a bank, and said they were trying to rob him.

Luke gets sentenced and does seven years in a maximum prison, and then some extra time in the federal system.

Not only did he have to do federal parole, he also had to do state parole. This is a guy who was a great student, had a solid family and had wonderful things happening in his life before he goes to prison. When he gets there he enrolls into a program that is an intentional discipleship and reentry program. Through this program, and the change that Christ had in his life, Luke never looked back.

Luke got out of prison and finished up his degree at K-State. Luke is now the Executive Director of a ministry that was birthed from the one that helped change his life. This ministry literally drops the recidivism rate from 35% as a state down to 14%.

Luke is one of the best friends I have, and I get to serve God daily with him by my side.

These stories are true tales of the power of change that we can introduce into the prisons through Christ and through discipleship.

Part
Three

Chapter Eight: P for Prepare

In this section we will work through each letter in the acronym PLANT.[1] We will plug in the formula, and a structure to PLANT churches inside of correctional facilities. Let's break down what each of these letters stand for. P is for prepare, L is for launch, A is for assemble, N is for Nurture, and T is for transition.

When you are looking at the planning portion of planting a church inside of a prison, there's a lot of variables that you need take into consideration. It's not just picking a spot, starting a study, and then just calling somebody. You will be jockeying for positions for very limited space, competing with different call-outs and other religions, trying to please the chaplain, and respecting the authorities of the facilities. Not to mention, in order for the prison to run efficiently, there are many different times throughout the day where there is no movement allowed in the facility, so that the required schedule such as count, and meal times, and any appointments with counselors and medical staff can be taken care of.

---

[1] The PLANT acrostic is taken from *Ripe for Harvest: A Guidebook for Planting Healthy Churches in the City* (Rev. Don Allsman, Rev. Dr. Hank Voss, Rev. Dr. Don L. Davis, Eds., TUMI Press, 2015).

So, now we will gently walk through the process of developing a Plan. To start with, pick a prison that you feel led to start a church in. Pray, seek council, and find like-minded people to start these steps with you.

When you identify the facility, call the chaplaincy and find out what they have going, and what you can get involved in. This will give you the chance to become more familiar with the administration and volunteers who are already active in ministry there. This way, you will also get a feel for the population that is housed there.

Start by spending time with the men and the women who are inside of the prison. You need to get to know them. You need to pour into them and let them pour into you. I'm going to tell you right now, it is not ever a one-way street. This experience will change your life forever.

The other thing that is important is collaboration. You should never approach any other volunteer in a manner as to say, "My idea is better, and you need to do this with me."

The very first church I ever planted was with the guys inside, and three of them are serving a life sentence. To be brutally honest, I probably grew more from the situation than some of them did. So really that's rule number one with planning: don't ever come into it thinking that you're going to teach them or you're going to give them something that they couldn't get from somebody else.

If you go in with the humble perspective that you are going to work together to build God's Kingdom, then you will definitely succeed. So, like I said you start with identifying what are the call-outs there, get involved in one of them, and start meeting with the men and woman who are incarcerated.

Learning what the prison offers, and what it doesn't offer, learning who is involved, and who the leaders are will help you start to plot a course. We need to go into the prison with a spirit of learning at this stage. The different organizations are doing amazing things. It takes a lot to be consistent over and over in a place that really brings no tangible return for the efforts given. There will be no pretty church building, no fantastic monetary return, and you will experience a ton of struggle and hurt.

But you will also change the direction of a life that was already standing with one foot in Hell. You will possibly bring life to a family that has been missing a husband and a father, or a mother and a wife. You will be a hope and light in the darkest of all areas. And you will be doing exactly what Jesus told us to do in Matthew 25. So stand with them and support and embrace those putting in the long hours for the least of these.

When you start seeking the people to build with you, don't ask who the leaders are, just watch and pray and soon you will see them. Take your time and watch for the people who are sold out to Christ, and willing to be teachable. Look for the servants, for the people who pour into other men and women.

When you are in the facility watch and listen to the conversations, the subjects, the content, and the way that they treat each other. You will pick up on issues like control and bullying. You will also be able to see where the respect lies and be able to navigate through the sub-culture that you will find inside of the prison.

When you find the ones you feel are right, start working with them, and start finding out what their dreams and their goals and their callings are. First find out how to grow with them into that calling. Ask questions like, are they being discipled, is there good spiritual maturity, and do they respect the authority over them. Find out the principles and policies in place that will help them get to the next step in their life.

Some prisons offer the ability to take college courses on biblical discipline and theology. Other places this is not an option. So you have to be creative when it comes to prisons. Some prisons are open to the idea of programs, and some are not. Seek out the resources that are already there and build on them. If there aren't any, well, hallelujah, it is time to build the foundation.

Once you have an opportunity to hold a callout, and you have found an open spot in the schedule of the facility, start the conversation about the who, what, where, how and when. Start digging in with prayer and working together for the bullet points of the mission. Not only on the outside, but on the inside also. Have them fast and pray as you fast and pray about the direction to take to achieve the goals you have worked together on. Such as, what church planting model to use, and how many people you can fit in the callout. What has fit best for me so far has been the Christ The Victor (www.ctvchurch.org) model built by World Impact and The Urban Ministry Institute. It is beautiful because you can take it and mold it to just about anything as long as you keep the DNA of Christ. It naturally comes with a great structure to teach the guys as they grow.

It doesn't have to be just this model. You can take a structure or skeleton of another plant and use that. You can add all kinds of things if you keep the DNA true. The DNA I speak of is the major parts to the service. The message and the communion, also known as the Word and the Table. Liturgy is also a huge part of the Christ The Victor movement. It teaches the guys about the Word and gets them familiar with passages that they normally would not read.

Once everyone is on the same page, and you have begun to build the structure of the service, start getting the members familiar with it. Have the church members inside start small Bible studies, with two to five people. Now, you've got to remember, we have to be careful because these men and women can get called for grouping. That is when there are more than two of the same race in a group. The Department of Corrections in any state doesn't like to see that due to the possible chance it turns into a problem.

Now is a good time to talk about situational awareness. This is having the presence of mind and always remembering that you are in a prison, and bad things still can happen. You always have to have situational awareness of where you are, and what is around you. You might not ever get hurt, and there might never be an incident. But on the off chance of a problem, watch how people act and how they talk to each other. Look for escalation of speech and flagrant hand gestures, and always trust your gut. If you feel something isn't right, find out why you feel that way. Ask the others around you if there is an issue, or if it is time for you to go.

So now that you have a team, inside and out, the leadership team on the inside are holding regular studies and discipling others, and the call out is starting to take shape, it is time to solidify the outside part of the team that has been praying with you.

Over the next paragraph I may hurt someone's feelings, and for that I apologize.

Chances are, the majority of the team that you start with will quit somewhere through the process. Life happens and will find a way to overtake the mission that is at hand. Others will quit because they think they are better than the mission, and the rewards are not as flashy when you deal with killers and rapists. Then there are others who feel you are doing it wrong and their way is better and they are not willing to compromise. Satan is going to try his very best to destroy the attempts of putting Christ in a prison, so be on guard and don't lose heart.

God did not give this burden to you just to go halfway with it. He is in control and will work out the issues. JUST KEEP GOING!

When we started we had a really small team, but our guys inside were amazing. I would recommend having at least three as part of your team who are able to work well with the team inside to help your mission to be as successful as it can be. What you don't want to do is fly solo and burn out when something happens. So, while you're working with the team inside you need to also be working with the team outside to spread responsibility among the group. You also need to hold yourself accountable to other people to make sure that you don't get exhausted and that you are not missing time with your family.

Then I would say sit down with the men and women who you are working with inside and out and set a plan of what you would like this church to look like in a year. Split the responsibilities amongst the team and give clear due dates for each task. However, with prison ministry it is important to be flexible. At a moment's notice, the prison could go to total lock down and the best laid plans fly right out the window! So be patient and walk with flexibility and understanding.

As you are building the final order of service for the church, make sure that the members inside take ownership over the service. Build it into an expression of what they want it to be, since it will be their church that they are building with you. We go in and out of the facility, but these men and women stay. Let's empower them to do something that is everlasting for the Kingdom.

When all of this comes together, it is time to formally Launch the service. We give these plans to God, and step out in faith as we launch the church.

Plan Review:

1) Pick a prison and call the chaplaincy
2) Get to know and collaborate with existing volunteers in prison and inmates
3) Prayerfully watch for leaders to partner with
4) Select and get to know your leaders
5) Get in the callout schedule
6) Decide on model of church and structure of service
7) Practice in small groups with your leaders
8) Solidify group of leaders on the outside who will work with you
9) Make yearlong plan with all your leaders on the inside and out
10) Maintain a flexible and humble spirit

Chapter Nine: L for Launch

We have put together a plan, we have the permissions in place, we have the people assembled, and the right people doing the right thing. Above all we are prayed up, and we are now ready for the next stage. It is now time to transition to the launch stage of PLANT.[2]

Prepare yourself ahead of time to let whatever may happen happen. Your launch may be climactic to the point that all the work leads to all the men and woman coming to Christ. The Holy Spirit may cut through the ceiling and the bars and flood the room with baptisms and Holy Fire. But then again, it might be anti-climactic and seem like it was just ok. One thing I know for sure is, not everything will go smoothly. You pray and practice and disciple and step out in faith, and then everybody forgets the plan, or the songs the band was supposed to play, or in some other way the service goes wrong. Maybe even some of your leaders end up in trouble and go to segregation. When these problems come up, it is the natural human reaction to feel slightly defeated and start to question your mission. You wonder if this is the right ministry, or maybe you even think the

---

[2] The PLANT acrostic is taken from *Ripe for Harvest: A Guidebook for Planting Healthy Churches in the City* (Rev. Don Allsman, Rev. Dr. Hank Voss, Rev. Dr. Don L. Davis, Eds., TUMI Press, 2015).

Spirit of God isn't moving fast enough. You are in good company, the first service is destined to be a little rough and out of step.

It might even be straight up awkward. You might just shoot milk out of your nose. People are going to forget what they're doing because they're nervous. They are going to forget what they were supposed to talk about, and ramble for a bit. They're going to forget that they were doing communion, and give a 20 minute testimony time in what was supposed to be a six minute slot. You will forget the cups or the crackers, and probably forget your sermon somewhere.

I mean, in reality this is most likely what the first service looks like when you plant a church anywhere, but it can be especially true in prison. As you get the first service in the books, don't take it too hard and don't have an immediate review. Definitely don't throw the hammer down on what we need to do now to fix all the dysfunction. This does not help things. This mission that you are on with these men is probably the most positive and spiritual thing most of the men and woman have done. I guarantee everybody is as nervous as everybody else. As much as it means to you, it means twice as much to the men and women who are incarcerated. Because guess what? This is what they have and they have poured their heart and soul into doing this just like you have and probably a little bit more than you.

Remember you're not dealing with people who have been raised in a church and are familiar with church functions and ministries. What you have is a beautiful mess that honors God in all areas. Just like a father whose kid plays in a game. The kid is trying his best, but doesn't quite know how it all works, but the dad is moved to tears watching his son.

I will say after the second service, they will take more responsibility and accountability for how it turns out. They will beat themselves up over what they feel is failure. You have got to make sure to be there with love and praise, and to reinforce the fact that nobody just gets on a bike and rides, it takes time. Take lots of time to love the leaders of this church, and to care for them. Some may never have been encouraged to do anything good, or even encouraged period. Tell them that it's more than okay, and it was awesome. Tell them this is part of the process when you start a new church.

One thing I have found to be true above all else in ministry is that it is always messy. We try to fix and correct things as much as we can, but ministry is run by people. People have emotions, hurts and pre-conceived notions. If we are honest, we know we all do. There is always a possibility for others to be hurt, or not engaged. So let us be ever vigilant to care for the hearts of the men and women we serve.

Make sure you stay positive for yourself as well. This is not going to be easy for you. You will feel like a failure, and sometimes like if you had done this or that better, it would be perfect. Guess what, it will never be perfect by our standards! But in the eyes of God, it is just what it needs to be. Stay strong, my warrior friends.

Once you get past the first and second service, you will see the men and the women take accountability for any deficiencies or mishaps in the service. They will do their best to work with you to make their church the best it can be.

One of the biggest things you need to pay attention to is time management, how to use the allotted time to fit the service in. In the world outside of prison, time management it important but there is extra leeway if a service goes over. In prison this is not the case. You are jockeying for a relatively small piece of time with a lot of different people and organizations. The chaplain will probably give you an hour to an hour and a half of time, and you need to respect the time.

The whole prison runs on a time schedule. There is a specific time for lock up and counting the inmates. There is a specific time for the meals. There is a specific time for laundry and showers. You name it, there is a time for it. Call-outs happen only at designated times and places. So if you have an hour and half, then you have to make sure that you get all the appropriate parts of the worship service together in that hour and half.

After the first couple of services, you will see which parts need shortened or lengthened. You never know, you might get up there and preach a message after 15 minutes of worship, and your sermon is 25 minutes then everybody is scared to talk, so they rush through communion and no one has a testimony. So each part ends up taking only two to three minutes, and you end up with an hour and half service done in 52 minutes. On the other end, there may be some people who ramble on telling a story that recaps the Ice Age and the dinosaurs, all the way to their coming to Christ through a drug-induced epiphany.

This is where discipleship comes into action. Take your members and run through what you want this service to look like, and teach them ways to relax and stay on point. Show them how bullet points can keep them in the lane and help them focus. Teach them how to breathe and pray. Have them run through the service as a team when you're not there. Empower the men and women to set the guidelines and to hold each other accountable to this.

Specific times for testimonies and praises are awesome, and if you want to do it every service, that's fine too. However, you will need to figure out how to make this fit in the schedule. First and foremost, you are there to have church. It is really easy to get side tracked with all the stories and stuff that goes on. We want to make sure that the members are getting well-fed. Jesus said, "Feed my sheep"(Jn. 21.17), and we need to make sure we are doing that.

After about four services, you should have a good grasp on what it look like and the corrections that need to be made.

As you're building up the team for preaching and teaching, you need to have people who can pour into the praise band also. There are phenomenal musicians in the prisons who need to be empowered and encouraged.

Some of the best worship experiences I have ever had were with the guys inside the prison. This part of the service is integral to the growth of the men and women in the church. Build up your worship leadership, teach them and disciple them. The musicians lead us into the presence of God, and there's a lot of wonderful musicians inside prison whose skills need to be fostered and raised to their full potential.

Work together with your whole team to create an environment that fosters growth and transformation. This will help your launch be all that it needs to be.

And when I say, "All that it needs to be", I mean all that God wants it to be.

Launch Review:

- Remember not everything will go as planned
- After the first service, encourage your leaders and give them (and yourself) much grace
- Pay attention to time management
- Readjust the service as needed
- Review with your leadership what went well and how to improve

Chapter Ten: A is for Assemble

As we work on building a church, there is an easy sin to fall into. Its name is pride. These men and women will put you on a pedestal, and guess what, you can get comfortable there. Don't! We have to be ever vigilant not to fall for that trick. Pastors and leaders all over get sucked into thinking that wherever they are serving is their ministry. I have been guilty of this myself.

You must always have great friends who will keep you accountable and check on you regularly. We are there to empower and grow the indigenous leaders who don't know they are leaders yet. We are also there to spread revival that will stay and stand the test of time. This only happens with change and growth from within the prison. If the source is outside the prison it will wane and fade. We have an obligation to bring them to Christ and to empower them to lead. We cannot do this by ourselves without a body of believers lifting us up.

The assemble piece of the PLANT acrostic covers how we bring people in to fill the church.[3] Be prepared, it is very different seeking out church members in a prison

---

[3] The PLANT acrostic is taken from *Ripe for Harvest: A Guidebook for Planting Healthy Churches in the City* (Rev. Don Allsman, Rev. Dr. Hank Voss, Rev. Dr. Don L. Davis, Eds., TUMI Press, 2015).

setting. There is no liberty to do any fancy or fun stuff you can do on the street to draw people in. We need to rely heavily on God (which we should do anyway) and be creative and strategic at the same time.

The one constant truth that is the same on both sides of the fence is that the church will grow the fastest and the healthiest if the men and women promote and believe in the church that you will be starting. The other side of this coin is they must buy off on us. This is a raw environment. If you come in promoting yourself or with selfish ideology, they will see right through you. If they do not believe in what you are doing and what you represent, they will not believe in the church that you want to plant.

However, if you come in with a genuine, loving and humble heart, they will love and support the mission with you. These men and woman are some of the most faithful people that you will ever meet. Be honest with them, and the majority of what you give back will be the same.

I have observed a variety of people run call-outs, facilitate Bible studies, and preach in the chapel services. I have also seen a variety of people do other activities in prison, not just spiritual activities. In any case, the adage is true, "People don't care how much you know, until they know how much you care."

There are a multitude of people who go to serve in prison for the wrong reasons, and will promote things that do not honor God. Let us not be them.

These men and women need to know that you care. Once they see that, and walk with you in that, they will tell the others in the prison, and this is the way to see change. You will start to see a little fruit, then a little more, and then something crazy will happen somewhere that sets you back a bit. This is ok. Remember the roots have to grow deep in the soil, and this takes time. And just like the roots, Christ's love must grow in the hearts of the men and women who you serve in the prison.

We must remember we are dealing with people who have been through traumatic experiences. There are multiple open wounds and they need to know that there is something real and hopeful as they wander through a place with a surreal environment that breeds sadness and loss. In this culture things are totally different. The majority of people who walk in this culture don't know how to have personal attachments to other people. Even when they do form some kind of a friendship, something so small as a honey bun or a five-dollar debt, could get somebody stabbed and beat up. This is the craziness that we need to step into with the light of God.

If we want to fill the church, we need to fill their hearts. We need to preach the truth. We need to preach love. We need to show them that they do matter, and that they are important. We need to show that they are not just a project we do or a box to check for charity. They will see and feel your heart for them, and they will forever love you like you do them.

If you have planned, launched, and built this callout with these concepts running through the DNA, people will show up. When we started the Christ the Victor church in the Hutchison Correctional Facility we started off with a packed house. The rooms could really only fit 20 to 25 people, 30 if we pushed it, and it was sweaty.

We started off awesome, but as time went on people fell off. Eventually things lose the new car smell, and the new car finish. This is ok though. What happens from this is you will know exactly who you should pour into for leadership. You will also find out who is in there for the wrong reasons.

If you will stay consistent and continue to empower the men and the women to be consistent with you, you will find that core group who will pull other people into the church. They will believe in you and in the church. This is where you will see the upswing in the attendance. Stay tilling, stay planting, and stay praying. There is a revival coming to the prisons, so we need to be faithful.

As long as you are pointing them to Christ, they will see and feel something real. Through this you will raise true leaders, and you will help usher souls into the Kingdom. The collateral beauty of all this is when almost everything is fake, and ingenuine and harmful, these amazing people will be drawn to the church stronger than smoke to your eyes from a fire.

The other thing you have to be on the lookout for in the assembling of the body is not to put people in leadership who are trying to lead people the wrong way.

This could come in a variety of shapes and colors. Such as, dividing the church on personal preferences of worship practices, or arguing over contemporary music as compared to traditional. Or even soteriology, and whatever side you find yourself on. As you build the church, focus on the primary doctrine of God, the Nicene Creed or the Apostles Creed. Let's build a firm foundation in the church and use Bible studies to handle the other topics.

Through prayer and fasting, God will provide the increase of people for the church. They will come and be curious, but at the same time pulled back and reserved. This is where we really dig into the nurturing portion of this process of church planting behind bars.

Assemble Review:

- Maintain an honest and humble heart
- Show the inmates that you genuinely care about them
- Don't get discouraged if people leave
- Stay consistent in pointing people to Christ
- Beware of divisiveness in your leadership

Chapter Eleven: N is for Nurture

Well, we've Planned, we've Launched, and we've Assembled. Now let's talk about Nurturing.

Nurturing is a very important piece of the puzzle, if not the most important. Just like we were talking about in the last chapter, it's important for these men and women to know that somebody cares about them, and not only about what they want to get from them. They need people in their lives who really want to see them not only succeed but know Christ on a deep and personal level.

This is the very essence of discipleship in my opinion. Just like us, every one of these men and women are unique and at a different part of their walk through life. Some know Christ, some don't. Some have never heard the Gospel, while others have been indoctrinated with a perversion of the Gospel. We cannot cookie-cutter discipleship as a blanket for everyone. Yes, there are a number of things that could be considered applicable to everyone. Such as, Bible studies, quiet times, prayer, memorization of verses, and even the twelve steps of sponsorship. Outside of this, you cannot do the same thing for every person, everywhere, every time.

People in these facilities come with their own set of unique characteristics. Some outside people can have trouble seeing through the layers to who they really are. Many prisoners are dealing with decades of trauma, and on top of that are living in an oppressive environment. These factors add up to people with hard shells to crack before you can start working on the root of the pain in the heart.

When you hold the services, be sure to include different people to serve in the various roles. There are many roles that need to be filled in the service such as ushering, welcoming, leading prayer, reading through the liturgy, or serving communion. All these different roles of service give you opportunities to raise the members up to learn the very tenets that represent a church service.

You need to be intentional about training the leaders to train the congregation. One of the biggest deficits in the church today is a lack of vertical to horizontal training. What I mean by this is we do not train our leaders to train other leaders. I have also been guilty of not making sure that the leaders I work with are trained to the best of their ability, so that they can train others to that point.

Here are some truths in the facilities that you might find. You're probably going to find out that the guitar player for the worship band has a problem smoking synthetic marijuana or might even be doing heroin. You may also find out that your lead guy for the church who has every point you want to see in a disciple, just so happens to have an inappropriate relationship with another inmate. You may find the greatest teacher inside of the prison, but they berate and control the people they teach! You just never know.

That is why the nurture piece of the church planting process is so important. Foster the congregation that God has given you stewardship over. Love and grow them into how God sees them. Plead with them until you have no tears left that they are very important. You have the opportunity that most people will never get in a churchy saturated world. You will get to usher a soul into the Kingdom of God and raise them into maturity. You never know what God has planned in the lives of these men and women. The next great prophet of the church could be sitting in prison right now, waiting for you to love and disciple them.

If we're honest with each other, the makeup of people in the church on the inside is not much different than the church on the outside. It is more obvious in prison because the quarters are extremely close. No one has any space to hide their true selves. Every congregation is filled with a variety of people who all have masks on pretending to be somebody that they're not, and will fight to the death to defend their false identity.

All the time we find out that great leaders have struggles with pornography, drugs and drinking, theft, extortion, inappropriate relationships, infidelity, and a slew of other problems. So really, prison is just a concentrated form of the outside world.

Your job as the pastor, leader, parishioner, bishop, or whatever you want to call yourself, is to nurture the leadership to nurture others. The people are our job. It is to look at the very "worst" and love like Christ until that man or woman holds the place of love in your eyes. This happens when you build them up and then everybody else in the church can see what it looks like to portray Christ. They see the glory of God in the transformation of the same people they live with, the very same people who may have been high right before church.

When you make other people's growth your highest priority, they will grow in amazing ways and it will bless you beyond what you could ever imagine. They will also learn to start caring unselfishly for the flock. They will start to believe that you really do love them, and the byproduct will be their own development in their spiritual walk.

What we are actually doing is taking people from a place of hurt and despair, from a place of distrust and no self-esteem, and helping them transfer into a place of adoption in the family of God. Through this system we are changing a brokenness that has plagued their families and helped propel them into prison. The majority don't know or understand what it's like to have functional relationships in their families or marriages. Through your actions, you have the chance to show these men and women the beauty, grace, and sufficiency of the mercy of God.

Once again, our responsibility is to take them from one place to another and not let them feel like they are not good enough to make this transition. It is a delicate dance of grace mercy and truth. So please be careful, we are working with souls.

We ended up planting two churches at the same time. I was stretched and torn, but I was not broken beyond repair and neither was the team. We nurtured each other and cared deeply about each other. We randomly checked for exhaustion throughout the team. Because of the hardships and our care for each other, we grew together as a team. Now we have a bond that is unbreakable. There are two beautiful churches that are functioning the best they can in a prison setting with what they have. That is because I took the time to work with these men and love them and then love the rest of the congregation with them.

Also, there needs to be consistency in the preaching schedule when you start. This is to get the overarching mission to stay on course.

I would maybe do the message three weeks a month for the first quarter. Then do two each month for the second quarter. Then step down to one a month for the rest of the first year. This way you can train the church to really be the best they can in all areas.

This may come as a shock, but the food in prison is not pleasant. Can you imagine that? So, any chance you get to bring in food that is not prison issued, do it. Have a meal with them just like you would if you were on the outside. If you are really serious about getting to know somebody, you sit down at a table with them and you have a meal together.

The absolute best though is when they put together a spread and invite you to eat with them. When they do this, they are sharing their lives with you. Let them do it and eat with them and love them. They will be so appreciative that you don't feel like you are too good for them!

Ultimately, what you want is to nurture these men and women until they feel confident and secure in what they're trying to do for Christ. Take the time to find out what your leadership team feels called to do. Always be on the lookout for that new man or woman who is trying to find their place with Christ. Ask the Holy Spirit to show you these people, and to show you how to be able to speak into their lives to help them grow into their calling. Embrace who these leaders are in the name of Christ.

Nurture Review:

- Include a variety of people in the service
- Train leaders to train the congregation
- Love like Christ, see the congregation as Christ sees them
- Keep consistency in the preaching schedule
- Bring in a meal to share

Chapter Twelve: T is for Transition

It is time for the final initial in this process, which is T for transition.[4]

I would like to tell you a beautiful story, if I may.

I had the opportunity to go back for a Christmas banquet two years after we started the church in the East Unit of Hutchinson Correctional Facility. When I was there I found that a lot of people didn't even know who I was, and it was awesome! The leaders who helped plant the church inside became the full-fledged leaders, and the guy who I handed the reins over to was doing such a fantastic job of empowering leaders that the church kept growing.

Now you might be thinking if we are talking about empowerment of the men and women, why pick a volunteer to have the reins? The reason is, The Department of Corrections will for the most part not allow a call out without a facilitator. They frown on unsupervised call-outs, due to emergencies that can happen or fights that may breaks out. That is why there needs to be a point person in charge coming in off the

---

[4] The PLANT acrostic is taken from *Ripe for Harvest: A Guidebook for Planting Healthy Churches in the City* (Rev. Don Allsman, Rev. Dr. Hank Voss, Rev. Dr. Don L. Davis, Eds., TUMI Press, 2015).

street. Either a volunteer or a mentor type needs to be responsible for that call out. So it was Troy who took the pastoral position. He actually took the reins on both churches that we had started at the same time. Then he and the leaders picked a pastor, so Troy handed it off to another man named Kevin who's an amazing brother also.

So back to the story. I got to go back and watch these amazing men function as a body and hear this great empowering leader Don Davis speak. We also got to eat a couple of meals with them and just have a great time together.

I also was able to listen to the story told by my good friend who helped plant this church about how it started, about my calling and his calling, and about how God worked to make the church possible. God showed up that night and the cool thing was I got to sit there and cry tears of joy listening to the beautiful future that God had in store for the church.

I will tell you about Troy. He swears that he is not a pastor, yet he leads the flock. He loves these members like they are his kids, and because of that love there are two churches doing absolutely awesome. Not perfect by any means, but healthy and thriving. We always must remember that prison is a semi-transient location, people will transfer around the state and hopefully be released.

Because I was able to transition out, more leaders were raised up. Who knows how many people would have never reached their potential if we would have not raised up leaders to step in and grow.

Some of you guys may not be transitioning out, or maybe you're the people transitioning in. Either way you got to remember that the church is not a function of you, and that we're not the reason that it exists. There should always be a point that we can transition out, and the church not fall apart.

We should always remember that this culture sometimes has a tough time looking for Christ because there hasn't been a good, solid representation of what we read about in the Bible. The other part of that same coin is when they do find someone that fits the position of what they consider that person to be, they get hurt. Sometimes to the point of never wanting to step back in the church again. It is not always the pastor's fault, but we have to be on point because we could really hurt them and honestly, really hurt ourselves and that's not healthy or good for either of us.

If you decide to transition you need to think about a few things first.

Number 1: If I'm leaving who's taking my place?

Here's the deal. You don't have to find some super spiritual, super mature person to jump into your position. Take time and raise them up into what the team needs. What you need is somebody who is godly, teachable, humble, and with a heart sold out to God.

Above all, a teachable person is the godsend of any ministry. Build them and watch them closely. Prison ministry can eat your lunch. Satan does not like when we are in the prison bringing hope to people who once were active soldiers for him. So be aware, and act as your brother's and sister's keeper.

Number 2: How do I chart the timeline for the
transition?

Once you have the person or people to take your place,
start putting together a plan for the hand off to go as
smoothly as possible. I have been responsible for a
smooth transition from leadership to leadership and
watched the church flourish. I have also had a bad
handoff and have watched it struggle because I didn't do
well with the plan.

Take a look at your timeline and break it down into
sections. Make space for your replacement to spend time
with the church members even before he gets the chance
to preach. There needs to be a compatibility with the
body of Christ, and a sense of love and respect to start
building before they just take over.

Let me give you an example of why this is. There are
major trust issues with the majority of the people who
are in prison. This is not only a childhood issue, it is a
systemic issue. All the people around them are telling
them that they cannot trust anyone or anything except
themselves. On top of that, there is overarching racism,
and the Justice System is not geared for your benefit. All
of this makes it hard to believe what our motives are.
There are some really great people in different jobs in
corrections, but there are also many who think that the
inmates are nothing but trash and the scum of the earth.

When you feel like this from the time that you are a
child, it forms your self-perception. We must be aware of
the culture and the emotions of the men and women we
serve. It is easy to railroad over people, especially if it is

in pursuit of our vision from God for our life. Let us instead love and cherish the people we serve.

Once you and the church are comfortable, start putting them behind the pulpit. In this process you might find that preaching is not their strength and that is ok. There will never be a shortage of people who can preach a message. However, it takes a special someone who can pastor and disciple the flock inside. If you find them, take the time to raise them up.

Next, start phasing them in as you start phasing out. There needs to be no confusion in the fact that leadership is transferring. There will be some who will not like the change and use it to attempt to cause disorder. Just remain transparent with all about the plan and which phase of the transition the church is in.

After a period of time, remove yourself completely from being the person in charge. This may be hard for you. You will love the church like it is your baby but letting go will enable it to grow to its full potential.

If the church starts to struggle, you may have the urge to step back in to help out. Instead, you have to let the leadership develop through the struggles in order to become healthy. Be the voice of reason and be the ear of understanding for what is going on, but don't be the action that keeps stepping in to fix their problems instead of letting them figure out how to fix it.

The crew and church will want to come to you with problems or with plans and directions for the church. Redirect them to the team that is working together in the transition.

When you come to the end of the transition time, you must gracefully step all the way back and have a period of time where you are neither actively or passively involved. This is not a forever goodbye, but it is a chance for all parties involved to run the church as they want it to be. This really is the hardest part, but it is also the most beautiful part. You get to see all parties involved operating on all cylinders in their calling of God.

Number 3: What do I do now that I am not in the picture anymore?

Now comes the fun part. We get to pray and start the process all over again. We now have experience that will help someone else plant a church in a different prison, or even outside of a prison. We can also be a solid pillar of support for a team that is struggling with a plant.

Now, let's talk about the other part of this. What if you do not want to transition?

After you run the church for a while, start plugging in other speakers and other volunteers to come take part in what you are doing. The best way to break the stigma and grow the churches are to let people see that there is a movement happening behind the prison walls with these men and women, and it takes a whole village to help raise them up.

Also, teach the leadership to be constantly training others to be able to do their job, and to step up into a position in a pinch. There is a spirit of "this is mine" that flows through the prison, and it becomes a place of entitlement and control. We have to constantly be on guard and fight this and teach them that our identity comes from God, not from what we do, where we work, and definitely not from where we serve.

That is why it is important to have a variety of people who are ready to do all the facets of the services. Build a rotating schedule to keep all involved in all the areas. The other thing this does is helps remove the stigma that if you preach or teach you are better than the usher or the greeter. It will subconsciously teach them to serve and to keep the spirit of a servant in all they do, and in all we do.

So, stay strong, faithful leader. Keep moving upward and onward. You are part of an elite team that carries the Gospel to ones who the world has rejected.

You are helping bring life and restoration to the ones who are called The Overlooked.

Transition Review:

- Choose a leader to take your place
- Chart the timeline for the transition
- Have the new leader get to know the church
- Start phasing in the new leader, and phasing out yourself
- Be clear with the congregation about the transition and what phase you are in
- Step out completely
- Pray and start the process over

Epilogue

The cold hard truth is that prison affects everybody. It is a cancer in society, because sin is a cancer. Unchecked, it will eventually kill you, and any good thing that you have. These prisons are an out of sight, out of mind attempt at a cure for our sin problem. Well guess what? It doesn't work, and it hasn't worked. It's actually just a spot to magnify the sin of crimes and get better at committing them. Our job as Christians is to be there to walk with these men and women into a new life in Christ, and to lead them in a way that not only brings eternity, but a redemptive life with their friends, their family, their community, and everywhere they go.

This is really a chance to see and feel what raw, unfiltered redemption is. Once you strip away all the pain and hurt from years of despair and self-abuse, God steps in and rips them right out of the gutter and places them in the palace of a King.

CT Studd said, "Some wish to live within the sound of church or chapel bell; I want to run a rescue shop within a yard of Hell." I've tried to make this the motto of my life. It doesn't matter if it's prison, on the streets, or wherever I can possibly be, I want to see redemption feed into the prison. I want to watch redeemed men and women come out of the prison.

I want to close this book with a story about a man named Kevin.

Kevin has done 20 to 25 years for kidnapping and robbery. He was young when he did this, and he really was not a bad man. Turns out he made a lot of bad decisions in the process of doing drugs. This sounds oddly familiar and personal.

These decisions have cost him dearly. In Kansas there's old law and then there is new law. Old law means you can do just about anything that is a person (against people) felony and end up with life in prison. Under old law any kind of violence towards somebody else or threat of robbery or the act, can get life in prison.

So, under the old law Kevin received over 20 years for his actions. While he was in prison, he became a solid Christian man. He was well versed in the Bible and was active in the church. This man was on fire! Somewhere in the process, he ended up with cancer that had no real treatment for it. The other problem was the medical facilities inside of the prison is not always the best or effective.

There was an experimental treatment that possibly could have been able to help him, but they refused to pay for it. On the grounds that they don't pay or pursue "radical treatments."

Kevin ended up on hospice inside the clinic in the maximum facility due to some extreme cerebral swelling. He went to the doctor and they were able to take care of the swelling.

When he returned to the clinic he was down to six months until he would be released from prison. He was getting so close, and he was so excited to get to see his kids and the rest of his family.

However, on March 24th, Kevin passed away. Six months before release. He died in the hospital after being transferred from the maximum security prison.

I got to spend time with Kevin. I got to pray with him. I got to worship in church with him and he was never sad. He was always excited. He was always praising the Lord and he was always on point with the power of Christ.

Now imagine this magnified by 2.5 million. All these men who are dying whether it is from cancer or just running out their time in prison, or even getting stabbed or overdosing.

People are dying in their sin daily, and without hope. We are called and chosen by God to show what real life looks like, to show what redemption and love look like on a daily basis. We need you to show this hope with us.

If those of us on the outside don't stand up and show these men and women who God is, who will?

Appendix 1: The Statistics

Trends in U.S. Corrections

U.S. State and Federal Prison Population, 1925-2015

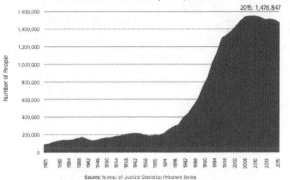

Source: Bureau of Justice Statistics Prisoners Series

International Rates of Incarceration per 100,000

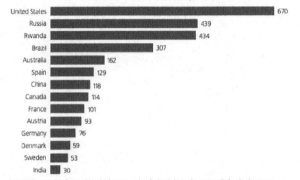

United States	670
Russia	439
Rwanda	434
Brazil	307
Australia	162
Spain	129
China	118
Canada	114
France	101
Austria	93
Germany	76
Denmark	59
Sweden	53
India	30

Source: Walmsley, R. (2016). World Prison Brief. London: Institute for Criminal Policy Research. Available online: http://www.prisonstudies.org/world-prison-brief

Lifetime Likelihood of Imprisonment

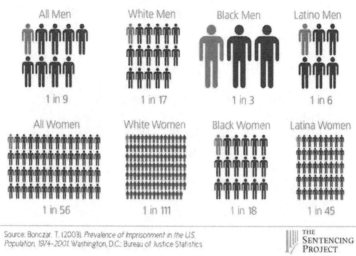

Source: Bonczar, T. (2003). Prevalence of Imprisonment in the U.S. Population, 1974–2001. Washington, D.C.: Bureau of Justice Statistics

THE SENTENCING PROJECT

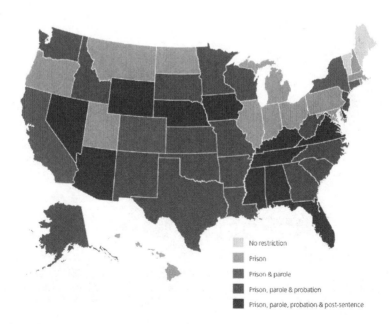

- No restriction
- Prison
- Prison & parole
- Prison, parole & probation
- Prison, parole, probation & post-sentence

State Expenditures on Corrections in Billions, 1985-2015

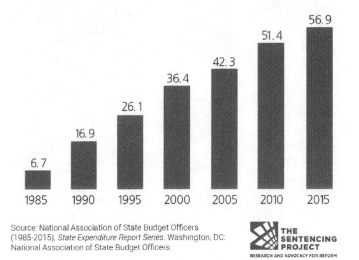

1985	1990	1995	2000	2005	2010	2015
6.7	16.9	26.1	36.4	42.3	51.4	56.9

Source: National Association of State Budget Officers
(1985-2015). *State Expenditure Report Series*. Washington, DC:
National Association of State Budget Officers.

THE SENTENCING PROJECT
RESEARCH AND ADVOCACY FOR REFORM

Number of People in Prisons and Jails for Drug Offenses, 1980 and 2014

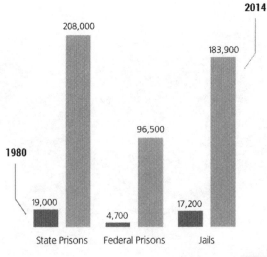

2014

1980

	State Prisons	Federal Prisons	Jails
1980	19,000	4,700	17,200
2014	208,000	96,500	183,900

Sources: Carson, E.A. (2015). *Prisoners in 2014*. Washington, DC: Bureau of
Justice Statistics; Mauer, M. and King, R. (2007). *A 25-Year Quagmire: The War on
Drugs and its Impact on American Society*. Washington, DC: The Sentencing
Project; Glaze, L. E. and Herberman, E.J. (2014). *Correctional Populations in the
United States, 2013*. Washington, DC: Bureau of Justice Statistics.

THE SENTENCING PROJECT

Appendix 2: The Scriptures

All Scripture from the English Standard Version (ESV)

Genesis 39:21 But the LORD was with Joseph and showed him steadfast love and gave him favor in the sight of the keeper of the prison.

2 Chronicles 16:10 Then Asa was angry with the seer and put him in the stocks in prison, for he was in a rage with him because of this. And Asa inflicted cruelties upon some of the people at the same time.

Psalm 68:6 God settles the solitary in a home; he leads out the prisoners to prosperity, but the rebellious dwell in a parched land.

Psalm 69:33 For the LORD hears the needy and does not despise his own people who are prisoners.

Psalm 79:11 Let the groans of the prisoners come before you; according to your great power, preserve those doomed to die!

Psalm 102:18-20 Let this be recorded for a generation to come, so that a people yet to be created may praise the LORD: [19] that he looked down from his holy height; from heaven the LORD looked at the earth, [20] to hear the groans of the prisoners, to set free those who were doomed to die,

Psalm 142:7 Bring me out of prison, that I may give thanks to your name! The righteous will surround me, for you will deal bountifully with me.

Psalm 146:7 who executes justice for the oppressed, who gives food to the hungry. The LORD sets the prisoners free;

Isaiah 42:6-7 "I am the LORD; I have called you in righteousness; I will take you by the hand and keep you; I will give you as a covenant for the people, a light for the nations, [7] to open the eyes that are blind, to bring out the prisoners from the dungeon, from the prison those who sit in darkness.

Isaiah 49:8-9 Thus says the LORD: "In a time of favor I have answered you; in a day of salvation I have helped you; I will keep you and give you as a covenant to the people, to establish the land, to apportion the desolate heritages, [9] saying to the prisoners, 'Come out,' to those who are in darkness, 'Appear.' They shall feed along the ways; on all bare heights shall be their pasture;

Isaiah 61:1 The Spirit of the Lord GOD is upon me, because the LORD has anointed me to bring good news to the poor; he has sent me to bind up the brokenhearted, to proclaim liberty to the captives, and the opening of the prison to those who are bound;

Matthew 25:36, 39, 43 I was naked and you clothed me, I was sick and you visited me, I was in prison and you came to me.' ... [39]And when did we see you sick or in prison and visit you?' ... [43]I was a stranger and you did not welcome me, naked and you did not clothe me, sick and in prison and you did not visit me.'

Hebrews 13:3 Remember those who are in prison, as though in prison with them, and those who are mistreated, since you also are in the body.

Appendix 3: Christ the Victor (CTV)

For More Information Visit: www.ctvchurch.org

Published CTV Resources (available at Amazon.com)

Christ the Victor: Book of Shared Spirituality

The Book of Shared Spirituality is our church year guide that contains prayers, lectionary texts, liturgies and other resources.

Christ the Victor Church: The Guidebook

The Guidebook is a thorough and in-depth summary of CTV's common identity and shared practices.

Raising the Banner High: An Introduction to CTV

Raising the Banner Book and DVD set contain teachings on CTV's core theology, worship, discipleship, and mission.

A Strong and Courageous Church: Advancing God's Kingdom through Discipleship and Leadership Development

A Strong and Courageous Church surveys the process of making disciples and looks specific issues related to each phase of disciple-making.

Made in the USA
Lexington, KY
16 November 2018